AMERICAN
ENVIRONMENTAL
HEROES

Collective Biographies

AMERICAN ENVIRONMENTAL HEROES

Phyllis M. Stanley

ENSLOW PUBLISHERS, INC.

44 Fadem Road	P.O. Box 38
Box 699	Aldershot
Springfield, N.J. 07081	Hants GU12 6BP
U.S.A	U.K.

Library of Congress Cataloging-in-Publication Data

Stanley, Phyllis M.
    American environmental heroes / Phyllis M. Stanley.
        p. cm. — (Collective biographies)
    Includes bibliographical references (p.) and index.
    Summary: A collective biography of ten American environmentalists, including
Henry David Thoreau, Rachel Carson, Sylvia Earle, and George Washigton Carver.
    ISBN 0-89490-630-5
    1. Environmentalists—United States—Biography—Juvenile literature.
[1. Environmentalists.] I. Title. II. Series.
GE55.S7 1996
333.91'16'0092273—dc20
[B]   95-38292
                                              CIP
                                             AC
Printed in the United States of America

10 9 8 7 6 5 4 3 2

Illustration Credits: Concord Free Public Library, pp. 14, 21; Sierra Club: William E. Colby Memorial Library, pp. 24, 29, 34; The MIT Museum, pp. 36, 43; Department of the Interior, National Park Service, George Washington Carver National Monument, pp. 46, 51; State Historical Society of Wisconsin, p. 56; Robert McCabe, University of Wisconsin-Madison Archives, p. 61; Yale Collection of American Literature, Beinecke Rare Book and Manuscript Library, Yale University, photo by Paul Brooks, pp. 66, 71; Earth Island Institute, pp. 76, 81; Courtesy of Barry Commoner, p. 86; Photo by John Millaire, p. 91; Al Giddings/Images Unlimited, pp. 96, 101; Photo by Robert McClintock, p. 106; Photo by Joyce Ravid-ONYX, p. 112.

Cover Illustration: Photo by Stanley L. Freeman

Contents

Preface

If I have seen further, it is by standing upon the shoulders of giants.

—Sir Isaac Newton, in a letter to Robert Hook,
dated February 5, 1675.

Whose idea was it to save America's parks, beaches, mountains, and forests for public use and enjoyment? Who uncovered the real story about radiation poisoning? Who first thought that improved sanitation and pure water could affect a person's health? Who warned the public about the dangers of using pesticides and other toxic chemicals? Who made us aware of the causes of pollution? Who showed the public how to make necessary environmental, social, and economic changes in the world?

The eco-heroes presented in this book come from different fields of study. Their lives and actions span two centuries, and they have made a significant impact on how we view our world.

There are some common bonds that link them together. Each one has considered himself or herself to be a part of the natural world, not separate from it. Each one has had a lifelong thirst for knowledge, and some have struggled against tremendous odds to get an education. Starting at a young age, each of them loved the outdoors, collected specimens, and recorded their thoughts in a journal. All of them have greatly advanced our understanding of the earth—whether it was to increase public appreciation of it, to conserve and protect it, or to educate others about it.

In the 1800s, Henry David Thoreau became famous for his writings and lectures urging people to attune themselves to nature. As a naturalist, he studied plants and animals by direct observation. He experimented with living a simple life, not being bound by possessions. Thoreau valued wilderness as a necessity for the human spirit.

George Washington Carver was an agricultural researcher who invented new uses for common plants and taught farmers in the South how to enrich the soil to grow better crops. He emphasized cooperating with natural laws. Based on his understanding of how plants grow, he taught soil conservation to prevent erosion and to improve crop production. Through his work at Tuskegee Institute he made a remarkable difference in thousands of lives.

All of our environmental heroes emphasized either preserving or saving the natural resources of our country, especially the wilderness areas. The concept of national parks grew from the wisdom of early environmentalists. John Muir and Aldo Leopold saw the devastation caused by overcutting the forests, overgrazing the meadows, tearing up the land by mining, destroying streams, and overkilling wild animals. Leopold's great contribution was teaching people about the "ethical use" (responsible use) of the land by maintaining the diversity of species and our planet's ecological balance.

Today we are encouraged to think of the environment in terms of whole ecosystems. The people who work to solve the ecological problems are called ecologists. Specific problems such as water and air pollution or the depletion of natural resources, such as forests or waterways, refer to particular ecosystems.

Two notable eco-heroes were responsible for revealing the importance of preserving ecosystems. Ellen Swallow Richards was the first woman in the United States to become a chemist. In the 1800s, she introduced people to the word ecology and she taught and raised public concern about ecosystems, particularly pure water and air. She raised the sanitary standards for homes (especially kitchens), schools, businesses, and factories. Rachel Carson did pioneering research that revealed the dangers of toxic substances such as DDT. Her 1964 book *Silent Spring* inspired the passage of the first environmental protection laws.

The present-day heroes whose lives have made a difference in the way we regard environmental issues are:

- Barry Commoner is the socio-ecologist who first alerted the public about the hideous environmental costs of deadly radiation poisoning. He did pioneer cellular research in the early detection of cancer and founded an ongoing research program to establish essential public safeguards.

- David Brower is one of the leading environmental spokespeople of our time. He led the Sierra Club battle that saved the Grand Canyon from being dammed. As director of Earth Island Institute, he has worked toward planetary restoration of waterways, forests, endangered animals, and native peoples which have been displaced by environmental destruction of their habitat.

- Sylvia Earle, a marine biologist and diver, pioneered deep ocean exploration and issued some of the first warnings about consequences of the destruction of ocean habitats. She has worked toward protection of oceans and further exploration of ocean ecology.

- Francis Moore Lappé was one of the first people to connect our planet's demand for meat and dairy products with the destruction of the environment. Her book *Diet for a Small Planet* was recently updated to present an environmentally friendly diet based on grains, fruits, and vegetables. She and her husband, Paul DuBois, have helped empower others to use citizen democracy to deal with environmental, social, political, and economic problems.

As we enter the twenty-first century, we are finally realizing that our resources are indeed limited. This is a time of ecological crisis. The new environmental ethic has blended all of the past struggles into one single issue. The environmentalist is concerned with the whole fabric of life on earth. Therefore, if people are a part of nature and the environment, then human problems such as hunger and disease cannot be separated from other environmental problems.

In the historical sense, it is interesting to note that the observations of early naturalists, such as Henry David Thoreau, led to the awareness of later conservationists and environmentalists who wanted to conserve the wilderness and to protect natural resources, such as water, soil, and air. Today, our eco-heroes are working on restoring and preserving a sustainable planet earth for future generations. We are challenged to "stand on their shoulders" and do new thinking about our environmental future as we examine their lives.

There is but one ocean though its coves have many names;
a single sea of atmosphere, with no coves at all;
the miracle of soil, alive and giving life, lying thin
on the only earth, for which there is no spare.

— From David Brower's
autobiography, *Work in Progress.*

Henry David Thoreau

Henry David Thoreau

Naturalist and Writer

It was an adventure . . . an expedition! Excitedly, the two Thoreau brothers, Henry and John, launched their homemade wooden dory on the Concord River in September of 1839. Although they were now in their early twenties, the two brothers had spent most of their lives either in or near Concord, Massachusetts.[1]

The night before, they had loaded their boat with a few necessities. Henry had his journal and his pencils ready. He planned to write down his impressions of the environment on each day of their thirteen-day excursion. The brothers traveled down the Concord River, and then up the Merrimack River to New Hampshire. Ten years later, Henry would self-publish his notes in the book *A Week on the Concord and Merrimack Rivers.*

The Thoreau family lived in Concord, Massachusetts. After Henry's birth, in July 1817, John and Cynthia Thoreau named him David Henry after his uncle David Thoreau. Because people called him Henry, he later changed his name to Henry David Thoreau. He had two sisters, Helen and Sophia. His brother, John, was two years older.

Henry's mother, an individual whose ideas were ahead of her time, introduced him to the natural world when he was very young. Sometimes, she cooked their dinner in the woods—a very unusual practice for those times. Henry took great delight in fishing, ice-skating, rowing, looking for arrowheads, observing all kinds of animals, and picking various kinds of berries. Sometimes he liked to whittle. He carved animals, whistles, and other small objects.

Henry and his sisters and brother began their schooling by attending Concord's public grammar school, where all grades sat together on hard benches. Although money was scarce in the Thoreau household, Henry was later enrolled in Concord Academy, a private school, from age eleven to sixteen. The academy provided an opportunity for advancement for promising young scholars.

The academy was only one of the many advantages of living in Concord. Except for short periods of time, Thoreau resided in Concord his entire life. For Thoreau, this village of about two thousand people was a microcosm of the civilized world. It had become a cultural center by sponsoring the Concord Lyceum—a place for public lectures on literary, social, and political subjects. Coaches traveling to and from Boston stopped in Concord every day.

Concord's natural surroundings of woodlands and waterways were appealing to Thoreau. He loved to wander in the woods and around the Concord countryside, observing and writing about the plant and animal life.

In the fall of 1833, he traveled fifteen miles to Cambridge and entered Harvard College. He spent many hours reading the books of Harvard's fifty-thousand volume library. One of his favorite books was *Nature* by his friend and neighbor, Ralph Waldo Emerson.

By the time he graduated in 1837, his high marks had made a good impression and he was invited to give one of the graduation speeches. In this address, he called upon his fellow students to "lead independent lives," and to be true to their own nature. He stated that greed and selfishness were causing people to destroy natural resources. He urged them to avoid seeking wealth, so that "the earth will be as green as ever, and the air as pure."[2]

After graduation, Thoreau did not know how he should earn his living. With his knowledge of the region, he was occasionally called upon to do land surveying. Although he had the skill, Thoreau did not consider it his true life's work. He did not want to follow his father in the pencil-making business, yet he helped in the family enterprise when needed. He tried teaching school in Concord, but quit after two weeks because he was expected to flog children if they were bad. Thoreau knew that above all, he wanted to live his own kind of life.

One of Thoreau's most successful enterprises began in 1838 when he and his brother, John, took over Concord Academy. They introduced many new ideas in education. The Thoreaus took students for weekly nature walks to observe animals and plants so that they would learn through discovery and firsthand experience.

Unfortunately, John Thoreau's ill health forced the academy to close abruptly in 1840. He died of lockjaw in January 1842. The school had been a highly successful experiment—many years ahead of its time.

When the academy closed, Thoreau's neighbor Ralph Waldo Emerson invited him to live in the Emerson home for a short time. To earn his keep, Thoreau did odd jobs like gardening and fence-mending. Emerson loaned Thoreau his books and introduced him to Concord's elite circle of writers and philosophers, who gathered regularly at his house. These people were known as Transcendentalists. Led by Emerson, they questioned society's materialism. They believed each person is born with an inner voice, or conscience, and those who live simple lives, close to nature, can hear the inner voice more clearly.

In their personal lives most of them wrote their ideas in journals. Thinking about what to write helped them to clarify their own insights. They emphasized making choices and decisions based on their own intuitions. Possibly these practices led Thoreau to write, "If a man does not keep pace with his companions, perhaps it is because he hears a different drummer. Let him step to the music he hears, however measured or far away."[3]

The close contact with Emerson became a major influence in Thoreau's life. Emerson encouraged Thoreau's writing by publishing some of his articles and essays in the Boston *Dial,* which he edited. At age twenty, Thoreau began the practice of recording in journals his thoughts about life and nature. As a naturalist, he noted scientific names of species, recorded life cycles, and expressed his ideas about the environment. He wavered between being a poet and being a scientist.

Emerson said of him, "It was a pleasure to walk with him. He knew the country like a fox or a bird . . . He knew every track in the snow or on the ground, and what creature had taken this path before him." [4]

People recognized Thoreau as he roamed the woods and fields around Concord. They remarked about the steady gaze of his blue-gray eyes. He walked at all times of day and night and in all types of weather, calling himself the "self-appointed inspector of snow storms and rain storms." He wore a straw hat, stout shoes, and thick gray trousers, sturdy clothes for climbing trees or walking through heavy brush. Under his arm he carried an old music book to press plants. In his pockets he had his journal and a pencil, a small telescope to spot birds, a microscope, and a jackknife.

In 1845, at age twenty-seven, Thoreau fulfilled a dream he had nourished for several years. He began an experiment with living a simpler life, one that was closer to nature—in the midst of a society that was becoming increasingly materialistic and industrial. After receiving permission from Emerson to use a small plot of his land beside Walden Pond, Thoreau built a small cabin. He wrote, "I went to the woods because . . . I wanted to live deep and suck out all the marrow of life."[5]

With the help of a few friends, he finished the plain one-room, ten-foot by fifteen-foot cabin in three months. On July 4, he moved in his simple furniture: a table, three chairs, a bed, and a desk. The cabin had a closet, an attic, and a fireplace. A woodshed and a privy (toilet) were out back.

"Simplify!"[6] was Thoreau's motto. He felt that people worked too hard to own things, and were still left unsatisfied with life. Now, he had plenty of time to read, to observe and listen to nature, and to write in his journals. In warm weather, he began the day by taking a swim in the nude. Before noon, he worked in his garden, planting beans, potatoes, and vegetables. Thoreau was living as close as he could to the natural world, trying to be self-sufficient,

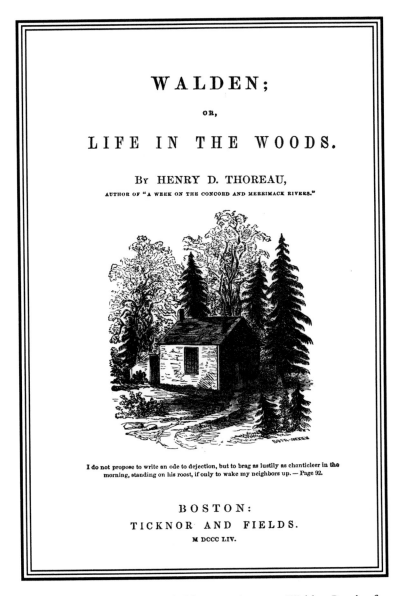

WALDEN;

OR,

LIFE IN THE WOODS.

By HENRY D. THOREAU,

AUTHOR OF "A WEEK ON THE CONCORD AND MERRIMACK RIVERS."

I do not propose to write an ode to dejection, but to brag as lustily as chanticleer in the morning, standing on his roost, if only to wake my neighbors up. — Page 92.

BOSTON:

TICKNOR AND FIELDS.

M DCCC LIV.

Henry David Thoreau ended his experiment at Walden Pond, of living closer to nature, after deciding he had many more lives to live and he didn't have any more time for that particular one. He published his account of this experiment several years later in the book *Walden, or Life in the Woods.*

yet his location at Walden Pond was less than two miles from Concord.

One day, during his second year at Walden, Thoreau went into town—and the constable arrested him because he had refused to pay his poll tax for the past six years.

Thoreau decided that he would spend time in jail to protest what he thought was the government's unjust action in the Mexican War. In addition, he was opposed to laws supporting the institution of slavery. Imagine his surprise and anger when someone paid his taxes for him and had him released the next day! To further express the ideas behind his protest, Thoreau wrote the essay *Civil Disobedience,* (which later inspired the use of passive resistance by Mohandas Gandhi and Martin Luther King, Jr.).[7]

Thoreau ended the experiment at Walden Pond in September 1847, after two years, two months, and two days. He stated that he had several more lives to live and did not have any more time for that one.[8] Years later, in 1854, his book *Walden, or Life in the Woods* was published.

After returning to Concord, Thoreau again sought refreshment in the wilderness and made two trips to the Maine woods. Commenting on the diminishing forests and wildlife, he wrote, "Our lives need the relief of such a background (the forest), where the pine flourishes and the jay still screams."[9]

Thoreau visited Maine a total of three times. Describing his climb to the summit of Mount

Katahdin in Maine, he was struck by its contrast to the pastoral scenery he knew around Concord. He considered the wild landscape savage and barren, and did not feel his usual joy in nature there. This experience caused his confidence in the renewing, spiritual power of wildness to falter. He did not feel at home there anymore. Was he in a foreign land?

Eventually, he concluded that the solution was *balancing* time spent in the wilderness and time spent enjoying the cultural benefits of society.[10]

In his research, Thoreau had explored the ecological succession of plant species through seed dispersal. His findings from his final research project were published over one hundred years after his death, in *Faith in a Seed* (1993). The succession of trees in a forest had been of particular interest to Thoreau.[11] To him the forest was a book waiting to be read. Based on what he learned about old forest growth, Thoreau thought each town "should have a park, or rather a primitive forest, of five hundred or a thousand acres . . . a common possession forever, for instruction and recreation."[12] It would be a place to refresh one's spirit.[13] Perhaps his writings influenced those who would later establish our spectacular national parks!

In 1862, Thoreau died from tuberculosis. He challenges us still with his ideas about simplifying our lives, keeping close to nature, and honoring the invigorating presence of wilderness on our planet.

John Muir

John Muir

Sierra Club Founder

Twenty-nine-year-old botanist John Muir stopped at an Appalachian Mountain vista to pick out a sample of the spring flowers for his plant press. In addition to the press, he carried only a notebook, three books, a sleeping bag, a few clothes, and some tea and bread for his excursion into the wilderness.

The first page of his journal was signed, *John Muir, Earth-Planet, Universe, 1867*, showing that he now considered the natural world to be his home address. He had decided that *living* was more important than *making a living*. It was the beginning of his impressive lifework as a naturalist and wilderness champion. He wrote, "I only went out for a walk and finally concluded to stay out till sundown, for going out, I found, was really going in."[1]

John Muir was born in the small fishing village of Dunbar, Scotland, on April 21, 1838. He was the eldest son of Daniel and Anne Muir. He attended the local public school until he was eleven years old. At school he learned English, French, and Latin, but at home only Scottish was spoken. The discipline both in school and at home was extremely harsh.

In 1849, the Muirs immigrated to the American wilderness in Wisconsin. Daniel Muir forced John to do backbreaking work on the farm and kept him from attending school. The Bible was the only book the Muirs were allowed to read. John was eager to learn and he secretly borrowed books from his neighbors.[2]

After many clashes with his father over Bible reading, it was agreed that John could read if he awoke before daybreak. John often started at one o'clock in the morning, reading or teaching himself mathematics based on what he had learned from his Scottish schooling and the loaned books. He had a special genius for creating small inventions to make work more efficient.

When he showed the neighbors his inventions they encouraged him to take them to the State Fair in Madison, Wisconsin. Finally, in 1860, against his father's wishes, twenty-two-year-old John headed for Madison with his inventions. He won an award of ten dollars at the fair.

In Madison, John was drawn to the university. He longed for an education.[3] After an interview with the dean, he was allowed to enter classes at the University of Wisconsin in 1861.

John looked and acted like an unschooled farm boy. He stood a lean five feet nine inches tall. His bushy auburn beard was untidy and his piercing blue eyes gave him a wild look. Also, he could not afford to buy more than one suit of clothes.

During his first year, he almost starved on his budget of fifty cents a week for food. The next year, he took a job and continued his classes. He especially liked his courses in botany and geology. His science professor urged his students to develop an awareness, or a "seeing eye," to probe nature's mysteries. He introduced Muir to the study of glaciers, which would later play a significant role in the naturalist's life.

Muir left the university after two years of study. Following a brief Canadian trip, he took a job in a wagon-wheel factory in Indianapolis, Indiana. In March 1867, a sharply pointed file slipped and severely injured his right eye. This accident turned him away from machines forever and back to his interest in nature.[4]

When Muir recovered his sight he immediately headed for what he called the "University of the Wilderness." His course of study began with a one-thousand-mile walk from Louisville, Kentucky, through the Appalachian Mountains to Florida. His travels eventually brought him to California, via the Panama Canal.

Soon after his arrival in San Francisco, Muir found his way to the Sierra Nevada Mountains. He finally arrived in Yosemite Valley in 1869. Muir made his home there for ten years, doing various odd jobs to earn a living. He hiked and explored the Sierras and climbed the imposing mountains while constantly studying geology, plants, and animals. His quest, both spiritual and scientific, was reflected in his journal writings.

Muir first attracted public attention when he published his findings about the glaciers in the Sierras. He carefully measured their current movements and concluded that glacial action had created Yosemite Valley and other valleys in the area. Muir's theory upset some prominent scientists. They believed that earthquakes and upheaval had created the Yosemite valleys. Muir noted that although the glaciers looked motionless, water flowed under them and carried soil and rocks down the streams to the valleys below.[5] He became an authority on glaciers in the United States and in Alaska.

In his Sierra travels, Muir often discovered that grazing sheep, which he called "hoofed locusts," had ravaged the mountain meadows. The sight of two-thousand-year-old virgin forests being crudely cut and burned to wasteland by loggers and settlers outraged Muir. He felt that these treasures rightfully belonged to all the people, not to a select few for private profit. He observed, "Any fool can destroy trees. They cannot run away; and if they could, they

John Muir spent ten years living in the Sierra Nevada Mountains as he studied the geology, plants, and animals of the area.

would still be destroyed—chased and hunted down as long as fun or a dollar could be got out of their bark hides."[6]

Like Thoreau and Emerson, he began to see that humans are only one part of the natural world and that each living part has a right to its own life. This contrasted with the widely held belief of the time that the earth was made exclusively for human dominion. Protecting nature from human destruction became Muir's lifework.

Although Muir had acted as a guide for ten years for many people who came to see Yosemite, he began to feel that he must do more to save these natural wonders for future generations. President Abraham Lincoln had signed a bill in 1864 requiring the state of California to preserve Yosemite Valley and Mariposa Big Tree Grove in the Sierras. In addition, Muir wanted the watershed areas surrounding Yosemite Valley preserved and managed by the federal government. He observed that state politicians were not protecting any of the public land from destruction by cattle, sheep, lumberjacks, and mining interests.[7]

By this time, Muir was already forty years old and friends were urging him to settle down, find a suitable spouse, and write about his experiences. In 1879, he came down from the mountains. He was introduced to Louisa "Louie" Strentzel, a musician and the daughter of a noted horticulturist. In April 1880, John and Louie were married. They lived on her family's ranch and orchard land near Martinez, California, about thirty miles east of the San Francisco Bay area.

Muir successfully managed his father-in-law's orchards for seven years. John and Louie's two daughters, Wanda and Helen, were born there.

Muir continued to take short trips to the Sierras, acting as a guide for those whom he thought might have the political clout to champion wilderness protection. In 1889, Robert Underwood Johnson, editor of an East Coast publication called *Century Magazine*, asked Muir to be his guide in Yosemite. As the two of them hiked and talked, Muir planted the seeds of his national park idea in the powerful editor's mind. Johnson encouraged Muir to write about his proposal and promised that he would use his contacts to place the national park idea before Congress.[8] The National Park Bill finally was passed in 1890, creating both Yosemite and Sequoia national parks.

True to his word, Muir had sent articles to local papers and written two features for *Century Magazine* about the wonders of Yosemite and the destruction that was taking place. He also spent much time making his Sierra notes suitable for publication. Muir's book, *The Mountains of California,* was finally published in 1894. It brought more visitors to Yosemite. He wrote, "Wilderness is a necessity. . . . Mountain parks and reservations are useful not only as fountains of timber and irrigating rivers, but as fountains of life."[9]

Muir and others who cared about wilderness preservation came together in San Francisco to form the Sierra Club in 1892. Their purpose was to preserve the forest and other natural features of the Sierra Nevada and to promote exploration and enjoyment of the area.[10] They elected John Muir to be the first president. Today, the club still fights for laws that protect the earth's wilderness areas and natural resources.

For the rest of his life, Muir spent most of his time persuading the public and Congress to preserve the wilderness so that it could be enjoyed by all. While on a western tour, President Theodore Roosevelt asked John Muir to guide him through Yosemite in the spring of 1903. Much to the distress of local politicians, the two spent three days and nights camping together with only two pack carriers and one cook accompanying them. Muir pleaded his case for wilderness preservation to T.R.'s sympathetic ears.[11]

As a result of his own leanings as well as some of the insights Muir had given him, Roosevelt later signed bills doubling the number of national forest reserves. He added five national parks, and established seventeen national monuments, including the Grand Canyon.

Muir's last preservation battle was over plans to dam the magnificent Hetch-Hetchy Valley, a few miles north of its twin, Yosemite Valley, to create a reservoir. Muir defended it because it was already in an established national park and it was a scenic treasure. There were less scenic sites that were available for public water reservoirs.[12]

Muir's disagreement with the land use policy proposed by Gifford Pinchot was at the core of the battle. Pinchot, who called himself a conservationist, was head of the U.S. Forest Service. He supported a policy for saving public lands—but for multiple use. This meant the use of public wilderness areas for additional purposes, such as timber, mining, grazing—or creating reservoirs. In 1913, in spite of Muir and the Sierra Club, Congress followed the "multiple use" philosophy and approved San Francisco's plan to build the dam in Yosemite National Park. One of America's scenic wonders disappeared beneath the reservoir waters.

The U.S. Forest Service and the Bureau of Land Management in Washington still follow the multiple use policy, although a few more restrictive management policies have been enacted recently. On the other hand, John Muir's Sierra Club called for the preservation of wilderness for all to enjoy. They did not, however, foresee today's trend of hordes of visitors from all over the world "loving Yosemite to death." The dispute still rages over the use of public lands. The U.S. Park Service still follows Muir's philosophy as much as possible by protecting the parks from public abuse. Over the years, Muir played a

President Theodore Roosevelt asked John Muir to be his guide during a expedition through Yosemite Valley in 1903. Roosevelt would later sign bills that doubled the number of national forest reserves, added five national parks, and established seventeen national monuments, including the Grand Canyon.

major role in preserving Yosemite, Sequoia-Kings Canyon Park, the Grand Canyon, Mt. Rainier in Washington state, and the Petrified Forest in Arizona.

In 1914, at seventy-six, Muir died of pneumonia while visiting his daughter Helen and her family. His memory is well served by his observation during his first summer in the Sierras, "When we try to pick out anything by itself, we find that it is bound . . . to everything else in the universe."[13]

Ellen Swallow Richards

Ellen Swallow Richards

The Woman Who Founded Ecology

The male students at the Massachusetts Institute of Technology (M.I.T.) in Boston stepped aside and let the young woman walk by, their puzzled glances followed her. Twenty-eight-year-old Ellen Swallow was the first woman to be enrolled at this bastion of scientific thought. She was pale and dressed plainly, in a dark high-collared, long-sleeved dress. She did not wear the puffed sleeves, bustles, and bouffant petticoats that were typical style for women in the 1870s. With steel-blue eyes looking straight ahead, she walked quickly and quietly. Her small frame was topped by black hair pulled straight back, which made her face seem even more pale.

The M.I.T. board had reluctantly accepted her

as a special student in chemistry. Little did they know that she would bring honor to their institution as the first female chemist in the United States, or that she would be referred to as the woman who founded ecology.[1]

Ellen Swallow had struggled over immense obstacles to obtain a higher education. She was the only daughter of Fanny and Peter Swallow, both teachers, who valued a good education for their daughter. Ellen was home-taught until she was about seventeen. She learned not only mathematics, logic, history, and literature, but also an appreciation for the natural world. In addition, her mother taught her how to cook, bake, clean, and sew. Her family moved to Westford, Massachusetts, from their farm near the village of Dunstable. Ellen was twenty years old when she graduated from Westford Academy in 1862. She excelled in science, Latin, and mathematics.

Ellen wanted to continue her education, so she worked for the next six years and finally saved $300 to enter Vassar College for Women. She scored extremely high on Vassar's entrance exam and was allowed to enter as an advanced student. When Ellen graduated in April 1870, she knew that her lifework would be in the sciences, preferably in chemistry. Courageously, she applied to M.I.T.— and was told that the board did not accept women.

Her attitude about this rejection was revealed later when Ellen recalled her father's reply after her mother expressed anxiety about overturning as their sleigh glided through snow-covered country roads. Her father had said, "Where any one else has been, there I can go." Expressing her own independent spirit, Ellen wrote, " . . . but adventurous spirits go beyond this and do what has never been done before."[2]

It was with an adventurous spirit that she entered M.I.T., where no woman had gone before, in January 1871. Ellen was given a desk away from other students, but slowly things began to change. She mended suspenders, bandaged cuts, and generally did other small tasks that many people expected of women at that time. Ellen found that by being useful in small ways, she made friends. She was convinced that more flies are caught with honey than with vinegar.[3]

What she was really doing was breaking ground for the hundreds of women who would follow in her footsteps. She supported herself, as she had at Vassar, with her fees from tutoring, and she worked for her food at the boarding house where she lived.

Always, Ellen's greatest ambition was to be useful to her fellow human beings. As she walked to school each day, she noticed horse wagons carrying uncovered food over Boston's dirty, unpaved streets, which were often flooded with pools of stagnant waste. She saw filth, disease, suffering, and poverty. Alleys were open sewers. Epidemics ran through the city. She now realized why less than half of the children lived to be adults. Ellen was determined to improve these conditions and to make others aware of the sanitation and industrial problems. To her the principles of science were not mere facts: they provided a possible vehicle for meaningful service to society.

After Ellen received her Bachelor of Science degree in 1873, she was invited to be the sanitary chemistry instructor, making her the first woman on the M.I.T. faculty. She worked as an assistant to her chemistry professor, who had a great interest in the new field of industrial chemistry. Ellen tested everything from shoe polish to baking powder. Even the food on school menus was subjected to chemical analysis.

She examined water, soil, rocks, and animal and plant life under her microscope. Her basic curiosity drew her to the rough-and-tumble natural world. Dressing for a survey field trip, she shocked her peers by wearing a bloomer-style athletic suit. She discovered two previously unknown elements in a rock and did extensive mineral surveys along with Robert Richards, M.I.T.'s young mineralogy teacher. Richards was charmed by Ellen.

Years before, Ellen had decided not to marry because she thought it would mean forfeiting her dream. Robert courted her for two years before convincing her that she would not have to trade her dreams for a dustpan and cookstove. They could each be pioneers in their own fields. At last, in June

1875, she became Ellen Swallow Richards. Their two careers did prove to be compatible.

They moved to a house in Jamaica Plain, just outside Boston. In the succeeding years, it became a friendly gathering place for students, faculty, and lecturers who visited the Boston area.

As applied scientists (that is, scientists whose work is involved with technological development), Ellen and Robert wanted their environmental knowledge to apply to their daily lives. They designed and installed a mechanical system of ventilation and circulation in their home. It was a radical idea for a house in the 1800s. They put in skylights and ventilated the gas lighting fixtures. Instead of heavy curtains, Ellen put green plants in her windows. She pulled up the thick, dusty carpets and replaced them with area rugs. She and Robert designed a hood for the stove and fans to pull the polluted air out of the house. Twenty years before the twentieth century, Ellen Richards had pioneered in the home environment the scientific engineering principles for air, water, and sanitary systems we know (in advanced form) today.

When M.I.T. built a new chemistry lab in 1878, the school opened it to both male and female students as a result of Richards' pioneering efforts. Previously, she had served for two years in a makeshift lab for women—without pay! She was not granted her doctorate because the chemistry department did not wish to award its first doctorate to a woman.

She had previously submitted a thesis and received a master's degree from Vassar. Smith College eventually awarded Richards an honorary doctorate in 1910.

In 1887, when the Massachusetts State Board of Health questioned the pollution of streams by industrial establishments and sewage from towns, it turned to M.I.T. to test the state's water for purity. Richards was in charge of the lab and did most of the tests. More than forty thousand samples were taken from all over the state during a two-year period. Richards sometimes worked fourteen hours a day and seven days a week to complete the testing. Her precise measurements and attention to detail established standards of water testing that are still being used today.

Later, using Richards' techniques and standards, the institute established the first sanitary engineering program anywhere in the world. Her book *Conservation by Sanitation* was published in 1911.

In her efforts to use chemistry to improve people's health and environment, she did hundreds of experiments, made speeches, and wrote papers and books. Her book *Euthenics—The Science of Controllable Environment* (1910) introduced the public to the science of ecology. In a speech in 1892, she introduced the inclusive word *ecology*. The term included not only the natural environment, but the domestic and human-created environment of an industrialized society.[4] She used the word ecology to refer to the relationships between organisms and their environment.

Industry leaders consulted Richards when redesigning

Ellen Swallow Richards often worked fourteen hours a day, seven days a week, to develop standards for testing water purity. These standards are so precise that they are still being used today.

factories and hospitals to provide for better ventilation, safety, and sanitation. Corporations hired her to test water supplies. She also did water tests for schools, businesses, and insurance companies. In her work in domestic science, she researched food additives. This led to the creation of the nation's first pure food laws.

Richards worked diligently to educate the public about environments made by people. She served as president of the American Home Economics Association. It was a group that supported bringing science into the home, with particular concerns for health and safety.

Her significant role as a trailblazer for higher education for women cannot be overlooked. Richards' own difficult access to higher learning motivated her to help clear the way for others.

Although she died in 1911, Ellen Swallow Richards' dream of bringing all of the sciences together to solve current environmental and health problems is still a current challenge. When new industries were beginning to belch toxic smoke and chemicals into the atmosphere, she campaigned for health standards and regulations. She brought environmental concerns about clean water, air, and sanitation, and pure food down to the individual and home level, as well as out to the societal level.

Today, the interrelationships of people with their environment are becoming increasingly important. Many environmentalists, both past and present, have come to their understanding of ecology through the study of natural sciences, such as biology. Richards' broader vision was to make all scientific research serve the health of the total environment, including the environment made by people. Ellen Richards can justly be called the mother of the science of ecology because of the breadth of her work.

George Washington Carver

George Washington Carver

Botanist and Agricultural Researcher

Peanuts! What about peanuts? It was 1921, and George Washington Carver had been given ten minutes to convince a congressional committee in Washington, D.C., that a tariff should be placed on imported peanuts. Carver's experiments at Tuskegee Institute in Alabama had yielded many products from peanuts. He wanted to encourage southern farmers to grow peanuts and he intended to create a market for them.

The legislators' eyes opened wider and wider as Carver removed dozens of bottles and jars from his battered suitcase. He pulled out candy, peanut milk, cheese, peanut butter, cooking oil, flour, instant coffee, shampoo, face cream, shaving lotion, paints, ink, and glue. When Carter finished showing his peanut products, they gave him a standing ovation. Later, Congress passed the tariff and placed a tax on imported peanuts.

George Washington Carver had come a long way since his humble beginning in life. As the son of a slave, his exact birthdate was not recorded. Historical records place it about 1864, near the end of the Civil War. He took his last name from Moses and Susan Carver, the couple who owned his mother. George's mother was kidnapped and presumed killed by the Ku Klux Klan when he was about a year old. The Carvers raised George as though he were their own child.

George was a small, thin child, too frail to help Moses in the fields. Susan taught him how to cook and clean, how to wash and iron clothes, and how to do other household jobs.

George learned quickly and when his chores were finished, he roamed the meadows and woodlands. Every day he brought home objects from his walks. Sometimes he collected flowers or rocks, sometimes small insects or animals. Susan insisted that his pockets be cleared of any live creatures before coming into the house.

As the years passed, George asked if he could go to school in Neosho, Missouri, a town about eight miles away. Even though slavery was officially abolished, the school in Diamond Grove was for white children only. The Carvers knew that George was intelligent and needed schooling. They finally allowed him to leave home to go to school in Neosho when he was about twelve years old.

Many people befriended George over the next fifteen years as he drifted around Missouri, Kansas, and Iowa. He struggled to earn enough money to pay for his food and his schoolbooks. He scraped by, doing laundry and cooking for others to support himself while attending elementary school, and then high school.

Finally, in September 1890, he entered Simpson College, in Indianola, Iowa. There, he excelled in art and science, especially botany (the study of plants). A year later, he entered Iowa Agricultural College in Ames, Iowa. After graduation, he continued his studies and received a master's degree from the school in 1896.

As a graduate-student instructor, this tall African-American individual stood out among the other college teachers, with his rumpled suit (always with a fresh flower in his lapel) and his high-pitched voice. His students loved and respected him for his laboratory, or "hands-on," teaching approach, instead of the typical practice of lecturing used by their other instructors. Carver took them on field trips to collect specimens, which they would later examine in the laboratory. To Carver, the whole world was a classroom. He told his students that all living things depend on one another in a natural network of relationships.[1]

Carver's writings about his soil and plant experiments were beginning to attract national attention and to bring government funds to Iowa State University. For almost a century, settlers had been cutting forests and burning the grasslands of America in order to plant the types of crops they had grown in Europe. When the land wore out, they moved on to another site.

Something had to be done to improve farming in the United States. Finally, legislators arranged for government grants to state agricultural universities to experiment with soil and plants. Iowa State had one of the finest labs, thanks to the work of Carver.

In his early thirties, Carver received an invitation from Booker T. Washington, head of Tuskegee Institute in Alabama, to direct a program there aimed at serving the poor southern farmers. Carver looked at his new greenhouse and fine laboratory equipment at Ames. This was the laboratory of his dreams. However, the Tuskegee offer was an opportunity that would fulfill another dream: that of helping former slaves who were trying to eke out a living on the eroded soils in the South. Finally, he made a life-shaping decision.

Carver arrived in Tuskegee in October 1896. He found that he was to head the agriculture department, the experiment station, and two school farms. He was also responsible for teaching several classes,

George Washington Carver discovered formulas for making many unlikely products from peanuts, such as shaving cream, cheese, and instant coffee.

landscaping the campus, and serving as school veterinarian. His laboratory was ten acres of bare land. There was no lab equipment.

Carver set out scouting the vicinity with his first thirteen students, collecting fruit jars, lamps, and old bottles and pans. Returning to their makeshift lab, Carver showed them how to make a test tube out of a bottle, a strainer out of a pan, and a little stove out of a lamp. Carver also had one microscope that he had been given when he left Iowa, which he used in the lab to great advantage.

The first term, Carver divided the land among his students for use as "living laboratories." Under his direction, they went to the school dump and gathered peelings and other garbage to start composting on their separate living laboratories. The students composted food scraps, grass, leaves, the stalks and vines of harvested plants, wood ashes, old plaster, lime, feathers, animal manure, and swamp muck. The decomposing waste left rich fertilizer for the barren land.

Year after year of cotton crops had badly depleted the soil. "The Prof" showed his students how to rotate crops. He explained that legumes take nitrogen out of the air through their leaves, and put it back into the soil through their roots. He suggested legumes such as black-eyed peas (cowpeas), velvet beans, soybeans, and goobers (the African name for peanuts) to restore nutrients to the soil. Farmers were encouraged to plant legumes to provide food for both family and livestock, and as a result, improve the soil.

To Carver, the whole world was a classroom. His view of nature was "that living things depend on one another." He studied not only plants and healthy soil conditions, but also the causes of erosion and depletion of the soil. He also studied the insects that impact plant growth.

In the early 1900s the boll weevil, a tiny insect, devoured cotton fields. Carver instructed the worried cotton growers to plant goobers. The farmers followed his advice and grew a bumper crop of peanuts—for which there was little demand.

Carver felt disgusted with himself that he had not thought about this problem. In October 1915, the Prof locked himself in his lab and started experimenting with the peanuts. First, he ground the nuts, heated them, and put them under a press. This process produced some easily blended oil.

Next, he took the dry cake left from pressing the oil, and added a little water. He tested it and found that it was full of protein. It had more carbohydrates than potatoes and more vitamins than beef liver. From the remaining ground nuts came peanut milk, to which he added a little sugar and salt. It later formed cream for making butter, cheese, and ice cream.

The marathon lab session of two days and nights had yielded twenty—later expanded to three hundred—products from peanuts. Among them were cardboard, paper, face cream, flour, dyes, cocoa, instant coffee, flour, salad oil, medicines, cosmetics, paints, beverages, foods for farm animals, soil conditioner, and glue. From this beginning, the United Peanut Association of America was formed. This group asked Carver to represent them at the 1921 congressional committee in Washington.[2]

In time, factories were built to make many of the peanut products. They used all the peanuts that southern farmers could grow. Hundreds of jobs were created, all because of the lowly peanut. Carver was pleased because the new interest in growing peanuts and rotating crops was also good for soil conservation, not only in the South, but in all of the United States.

The experimental fields at Tuskegee were so successful that Carver set up Saturday teaching sessions for the local farmers to show them how to grow thriving plants of all kinds. Eventually, he and his students built a wagon for traveling to outlying villages or farms to spread the information. They took seeds and samples of various plants. Carver taught them new methods of working the soil. He also demonstrated how to make cowpea pancakes, mashed cowpea meat loaf, roasted cowpeas, and even a drink that tasted like coffee.

For forty-seven years, Carver taught, wrote, and experimented in his laboratory at Tuskegee. He created 118 uses for sweet potatoes, including over twenty different varieties as foods. He also proposed general products such as alcohol, library paste, medicine, synthetic silk, and writing ink.

Carver died in January 1943. Today, the George Washington Carver Museum on the Tuskegee campus holds some of his paintings, his vegetable specimens, and his samples of products derived from peanuts, sweet potatoes, sand, and feathers. In 1951, the George Washington Carver National Monument was built near the Missouri farm where he was born.[3]

It has been said that his inner strength came from his relationship with the earth itself. He wrote that earth is "not just a treasure house to be ransacked and plundered and to be profited from. [It is] our home and a place of beauty and mystery and God's handiwork."[4]

Aldo Leopold

Aldo Leopold
Father of American Wildlife Conservation

The deep throaty howl of a wolf came rumbling through the blackness of night. Twenty-five-year-old Aldo Leopold was leading a group of ranger trainees. They had camped on the rim of a mountain in New Mexico Territory. Leopold knew the wolf's howl meant something different to the hunter, to the deer, to the cowhand, and perhaps to the mountain itself. What did it mean to the mountain? He thought, "Only the mountain has lived long enough to listen objectively to the [howl] of a wolf."[1]

In the chilly air, he was aware of the dawning of a new day. The rangers began to map out two more square miles of wilderness. About noon, the rangers stopped to rest. What happened next permanently changed Leopold's outlook on life itself. As the rangers rested, they spied a mother wolf and her cubs . . . and fired on them.

In his essay *Thinking Like a Mountain,* Leopold wrote, "The old wolf was down . . . We reached [her] in time to watch a fierce green fire dying in her eyes. I realized then, and have known ever since, that there was something new to me in those eyes—something known only to her and to the mountain."[2]

Leopold goes on to say that because cattle farmers, sheep herders, and hunters killed all of the wolves in that territory, many mountains were wolfless. A wolfless mountain has a maze of deer trails. The deer eat every edible bush and seedling. They strip every edible tree to the height of a saddle horn. In the end, the mountain is strewn with the bones of a starved deer herd. The deer may be replaced over the years, but the land erodes and becomes a naked desert. "Hence, we have dustbowls, and rivers washing the future into the sea."[3]

Aldo was the son of Carl and Clara Leopold, an outdoors-loving German family. Born in Burlington, Iowa, in 1887, he was the eldest of four children. When he was quite young, Aldo's father taught him selective game hunting. This included limiting the number of deer or ducks killed for food. He was taught never to shoot any creature just to show off his marksmanship. Part of his training was learning to identify various birds. He often visited the wetlands near his home to observe the birds and other wild-life. Starting at age ten, he kept a daily journal of his observations. The journal-writing habit remained with him all his life.

After completing most of his education in Burlington, Aldo enrolled in Lawrenceville (N.J.) Preparatory School in 1904. He then entered Yale University's Sheffield Science School, where he received his degree in 1908. A year later, he earned a master of forestry degree from the newly established Yale School of Forestry and was immediately hired as a forester.

Aldo was excited when the U.S. Forest Service assigned him to the recently created Apache National Forest in Arizona Territory. At last he was free to pursue his enthusiasm and curiosity about the natural world.

In 1911, he became a supervisor in the Carson National Forest in New Mexico. He headed a small group of rangers whose mission was to explore the forest's vast roadless wilderness. It was there that he had his life-changing experience with the killing of the mother wolf. The experience was recorded years later in his book *A Sand County Almanac*. Leopold explained his "land ethic" in this small volume of essays. It was published one year after his death in 1949. The book outlines many of the goals of to-day's environmental movement.

Leopold's fifteen years in the Southwest brought

him personal satisfaction and a measure of professional success. In 1912, at age twenty-five, he married Estella Bergere, daughter of an old Spanish family. They had a family of two sons and three daughters.

It was not until the 1920s that Leopold's land ethic became clear to him. He explained that an action is right when it preserves the biotic community—the ecosystem of an area. It is wrong when it destroys the ecosystem.[4]

For example, the wolves and mountain lions in Arizona's Kaibab Plateau were killed as part of a game management program. The deer herds expanded rapidly, but without their predators, they outgrew their habitat and starved. The mountain became barren. From this experience, Leopold drew an important lesson: a species cannot be understood or protected apart from its habitat.

He wrote many articles and focused public attention on the importance of maintaining ecosystem balance and diversity—or variety of species—in the natural world. He initiated wildlife reform in the Forest Service and in the public eye. Starting with seven hundred thousand acres called the Gila National Wilderness Area, he eventually helped to preserve 20 million acres of wilderness in the Southwest. In 1924, Leopold accepted a position in the main research facility of the Forest Service in Madison, Wisconsin.

His book *Game Management* was published in 1933. That same year he was appointed chairperson

Aldo Leopold believed that nature must be protected and preserved rather than exploited for short-term financial gains.

of the newly established Game Management Department at the University of Wisconsin in Madison. He established ecological science in the college curriculum.

He taught his students that an ecosystem is like a pyramid. It starts with the sun's energy acting on the water, air, soil, and plants. The energy flows through the various food chains on each level of the pyramid. One level contains the insects and animals that depend upon plants for food (the herbivores). The next higher level includes the animals that eat both plants and smaller animals (omnivores). At the top of the pyramid are meat-eating carnivores.[5]

The reason for the pyramid metaphor is to show the sizes of the steps. It takes a greater number of plants at the base to support all of the other levels. If the plants all die, all of the food chains collapse.

Leopold practiced his beliefs about restoring land that the early settlers had depleted (worn out). He purchased a farm near Madison in a "sand county" in 1935. The land there had been logged clear, over-grazed, and left as barren as a desert. The Leopold family mended the land by planting trees and en-riching the soil with nutrient-rich plants, such as legumes.

Leopold and others founded the Wilderness Society, an organization dedicated to preserving the natural world, in 1935. As a result of his teaching about wildlife and game management, Leopold is widely recognized as the father of wildlife conservation in America.

It is interesting to note the changes that occurred in Leopold's thinking about the natural world during his lifetime. As he grew older he began to realize that wildlife management was more of a way to restore and maintain balance in an ecosystem rather than a way to produce surplus animals for hunting. He no longer viewed the wilderness as recreational ground for hunting, but as a valued natural resource.

The major objective in Leopold's writing and teaching became the raising of people's awareness of the land's health. Healty land has the capacity for self-renewal. Sick land does not have that capacity.

Like John Muir, Leopold urged Congress to preserve roadless wilderness which could only be reached by backpacking or canoeing. In his lectures he taught that without wild areas to serve as a basis for comparison, people may eventually lose sight of what healthy land is. Each biotic community is different, therefore a wilderness of each type of land is needed. Wilderness provides the only hope of saving the large carnivores from extinction. Even the national parks have proved to be too small as reserves for animals that roam great distances. Leopold understood that as wilderness areas are destroyed all over the plant, the value of nature's laboratory increases.

The crux of Leopold's land ethic was that diversity in nature must be restored and preserved rather than "managed" for short-term gains. Today, we might find an example in the rain forests of the Olympic Mountains in Washington that are being clear-cut for short-term profit. The result is the same whether on public or private land. When ancient ecosystems are destroyed, the land is usually left barren.

Like John Muir, Leopold was opposed to the multiple use of natural resources. He taught his students that the wilderness is a laboratory for the study of land-health and that saving one part of the environment should not include destroying another part. However, the U.S. Forest Service embraced the idea of multiple use.

Leopold thought that people needed to develop an "ecological conscience." He believed the role of humans must change from being conquerors to being citizens of a biotic community. This citizenship implies respect for fellow human beings as well as for plants and animals. Leopold stressed that human beings are only one part of the great pyramid of life. He wrote, "Land ecology discards at the outset the fallacious notion that the wild community is one thing, the human community another."[6]

Early conservationists had campaigned to preserve land for future wilderness areas. John Muir wrote, "When we try to pick out anything by itself, we find it hitched to everything else in the universe."[8] Leopold contributed the concept of a land ethic: preserving the balance and variety of species, suggesting that we "learn to think like a mountain."

All of these writers and thinkers influenced the public and the Congress. That led to the passage of the National Wilderness Act in 1964. Wilderness areas are still being preserved under this congressional act.

Rachel Carson

Rachel Carson

Warned Planet Earth of a "Silent Spring"

She was about to sound an alarm! After five years of hard research, Carson began her book with a disturbing fable: "There was once a town in the heart of America where all life seemed to live in harmony with its surroundings." She described how a "strange blight" made everything change. Animals began to sicken and die. "There was a strange stillness. The birds, for example—where had they gone? . . . It was a spring without voices."[1]

It was a quiet beginning for *Silent Spring*, a book that provoked loud controversy among farmers, government officials, business interests, and the public. Author Rachel Carson went on to point out that all of the dire incidents in this mythical town had really happened in many different towns in America.

She explained that poisonous chemicals such as DDT were being sprayed on fields of grain and vegetables. These poisons build up in plants and animals. They reach rivers and lakes, where they endanger the fish, then the birds—and finally the humans who eat the fish. She pointed out how harmful pesticides dangerously threaten the balance of nature and all life. People who read these dire warnings had thought they were being protected by the government health agencies. Those who had not read her three previous books wondered, "Who is Rachel Carson?"

She was the youngest of three children born to Robert and Maria Carson on May 27, 1907. The family farm was near Springdale, in western Pennsylvania. Maria Carson was a teacher before her marriage. She taught Rachel at home for much of her early schooling because they did not have transportation to school for much of the winter.

After she won a story-writing contest at age ten, Rachel was inspired to keep writing. Her high school teachers thought she might have a career as an author. As it turned out, she became a scientist with the pen of a poet. She received a scholarship to attend Pennsylvania College for Women, and she graduated in 1928 with high honors.

During her second year in college, Rachel had become fascinated with biology during a required science course. She especially liked marine biology. After much thought, she changed her major from

English to science. Rachel commented, "Biology has given me something to write about. I will try in my writing to make animals in the woods or waters . . . as alive to others as they are to me."[2]

In 1928, she received a summer study fellowship and became a research assistant at the Marine Biological Laboratory (now the Oceanographic Institute) at Woods Hole, Massachusetts.

It is easy to picture Carson's soft brown hair billowing in the breeze and her eyes sparkling as she arrived at Woods Hole. On her boat trip she had experienced the ocean for the first time. All her life she had read and dreamed about it. For the rest of her life, Carson was never far away from the Atlantic coastal waters. At Woods Hole she met the foremost authorities on oceanographic science. She spent several summers there as she continued her studies at Johns Hopkins University in Baltimore. After earning her master's degree at Johns Hopkins in 1932, she became an instructor.

Meanwhile, her personal life was not easy. Her family had moved to Baltimore to be near her. When her father died in 1935 and her sister died the next year, Carson was the sole support for her mother and two nieces. To earn additional income, she started writing articles on fisheries for the *Baltimore Sun.* She also wrote radio broadcasts on undersea life for the Bureau of Fisheries.

After Carson passed a government exam, the Bureau of Fisheries (later part of the Fish and

Wildlife Service) offered her a job as a marine biologist. Carson was employed there from 1935 to 1949. For three years she served as chief editor for all of the U.S. Fish and Wildlife publications.

She continued to write about the sea in her leisure time. Her first book, *Under the Sea-Wind,* was published in 1941—two weeks before the United States entered World War II. The nation's attention was focused elsewhere. The book was not a success until it was re-released in 1952. She wrote, "To stand at the edge of the sea, to sense the ebb and the flow of the tides, to feel the breath of a mist moving over a great salt marsh, to watch the flight of shore birds that have swept up and down the surf lines of the continents for untold thousands of years . . . is to have knowledge of things that are as nearly eternal as any earthly life can be."[3]

By 1951, she had finished *The Sea Around Us.* It was an instant success that changed her life. It stayed on *The New York Times* best-seller list for eighty-six weeks and was translated into more than thirty languages. Ultimately, it sold over a million copies. She became famous internationally as a marine author.

Royalties from the book and her lectures allowed her to quit her government job at the bureau to spend more time writing and lecturing. Although she was poised under the spotlight, Carson was basically shy and soft-spoken. She did not enjoy speaking in public.

(When *The Sea Around Us* was later revised in

Rachel Carson spent many hours in the laboratory studying the effects of poisonous chemicals on ocean life.

1961, Carson warned of the danger of dumping radioactive waste into the ocean. "Once radioactive elements have been deposited at sea they are irretrievable. The mistakes that are made now are made for all time."[4])

Carson loved to spend quiet summers at a cottage she had built on the coast of Maine. From that vantage point, she was a strong advocate for protecting selected parts of the seashores as wilderness. At that time only about 6 percent of the Atlantic and Gulf Coast shorelines remained in public hands. In an article written for *Holiday* magazine, she stated, "Somewhere we should know what was nature's way; we should know what the earth would have been had not man interfered."[5]

In 1958, a letter from her friend, Olga Huckins described the devastation that occurred on her private wildlife sanctuary. Birds and animals had died when the state of Massachusetts ordered aerial spraying of insecticide in an attempt to control the mosquitoes. The letter moved Carson to investigate the use of insecticides.

She launched an extensive search for evidence about the biological and physical effects of chemical pesticides. She received some assistance from a broad circle of experts and scientists. The more she learned as she pooled all of the findings, the more alarmed she became. She said, "What I discovered was that everything which meant most to me as a naturalist was being threatened."[6]

She found that the use of chemicals to combat farm insect pests coincided with the rise of large-scale farming in the United States. With new technology, farmers had increased production by growing specialized crops, and swarms of insects flourished on those crops. Farmers, encouraged by the Department of Agriculture, had welcomed the introduction of DDT. Chemical manufacturers promised major advances in public health and agricultural production without concern about the long-term effects of its use.

Farmers stopped using the more gradual biological controls such as the predator-prey remedy or the rotation of crops. The chemicals provided a quick fix. Safety tests had been conducted by the chemical manufacturers, who had an interest in approving the chemicals so they could make a profit by selling them.

When Carson wrote about her findings, the article was turned down by several magazines. She decided to turn her work into a book. Although she had expected to complete her research in a year, she ended up spending five years on the project. Carson never could have predicted the consequences of her carefully-written book.

Carson combined a cool analytical mind and eloquent writing to deliver her message. She related the use of harmful chemicals to a basic threat to both human health and the whole ecosystem. When her research was published as *Silent Spring* (1962), it sent shock waves through the public. The battle lines were drawn. The lobbyists for chemical companies and the Department of Agriculture became the leading defenders of insecticides. They attacked Rachel Carson and tried to convince everyone that her findings were incorrect and that she was a troublemaker.

Carson cited many case studies when defending her research. One disaster claiming headlines at the time was an incident at a Memphis, Tennessee, chemical plant. The plant produced an insecticide that had contaminated the lower Mississippi River and killed five million fish. She found it tragic that the earth, and eventually the human population, too, was being poisoned. When public health became an issue, the chemical companies quietly paid lobbyists to influence legislation. Carson wrote, "[The insecticides] have immense power . . . to enter into the most vital processes of the body and change them in sinister and often deadly ways . . . they destroy the very enzymes whose function is to protect the body from harm . . . and they may initiate in certain cells the slow and irreversible change that leads to malignancy."[7]

In 1963 President Kennedy established a special panel of scientists to investigate Carson's claims. They found her to be 100 percent correct. She testified before a congressional committee that same year. Although she was not opposed to selective use of chemicals, she made specific recommendations about the regulation and use of harmful insecticides.

Rachel Carson had struggled for four years, often in great pain, knowing of her own fatal malignancy. She was determined to finish her powerful book. After completing it, often in great pain, she died of cancer in April 1964. Six years went by before the laws regulating the use of harmful pesticides were passed. Congress formed the Environmental Protection Agency (EPA), but enforcement of the pesticide laws remained lax well into the 1980s. Carson had insisted, "Trusting so-called authority is not enough. A sense of personal responsibility is what we desperately need."[8] It was personal commitment to the common good that led her to inform the public of her scientific findings.

The end of the story is not yet written. Increasing amounts of toxic chemicals and radioactive wastes are being produced around the world today. A solution to the storage of radioactive waste has escaped us. Who will take personal responsibility? Carson's writings about the sea revealed how all life is connected. *Silent Spring* helped to launch a new environmental consciousness. Through her work, Carson indicated how the future of all life depends upon our actions today.

David Brower

David Brower

Mountaineer, Activist, and Environmentalist

On a February day in 1936, David Brower and four Sierra Club companions were making a first-ever winter ascent up glacial Mount Lyell—the highest peak in Yosemite National Park, California. A full day's cross-country skiing took them to a windy snow camp two thousand feet above the timberline on the perilous mountain. The next morning when hurricane-like winds developed, they took off their skis. The half-frozen climbers crept toward the summit, digging in hands and toes for anchorage across the icy steep ridge of the glacier.

Finally, they left the wind far below as they reached the top about noon, still securely roped together. David stood up to inhale the thin, chilled air. He took in the 360-degree, top-of-the-world view. The vast alpine beauty of the top of the mountain peaks engulfed him. It was a familiar reaction for Brower. Now in his twenties, he already had thirty-three first ascents in the Sierras to his credit. Later, he would make seventy first ascents—meaning that he was the first person on record to have climbed each of those peaks. He says, "Mountain climbing taught me that courage and a strong determination can overcome enormous odds."[1]

Perhaps the image of those views from the top fed his unwavering passion to preserve such wild places for future generations. Little did he dream that his dedication to that cause would bring furious verbal attacks in later years. In his ardor for trees, birds, butterflies, canyons, rivers, and high places of the earth—such as mountains—Brower has acquired the reputation of rushing relentlessly toward his goals, sometimes forgetting to observe society's rules and regulations.

Brower's love for the mountains and the surrounding wilderness started early in his life. When he was six years old, the Brower family took their 1916 Maxwell automobile over primitive one-lane dirt roads to their favorite camping sites in the Sierras. (What was a four-day trip from their Berkeley home is now a four-hour drive on a freeway.)

The Brower family consisted of his parents, Ross

and Mary Grace, and their four children. David, their third child, was born in 1912. He spent many boyhood hours in the Berkeley hills near the University of California. His father, an engineer, was an instructor there. He was formally educated in Berkeley until he was about seventeen years old.

As a young person, David spent several summers leading hiking groups in the Sierras. Like John Muir, he was a bright student of forestry and biology, but like Muir, he quit college after about two years and headed for the "University of the Wilderness." However, one difference in their experiences was that Brower's Sierra wilderness turned out to be somewhat more occupied than Muir's—particularly Yosemite Valley, where he held intermittent odd jobs.

When he moved back to Berkeley in 1933, David met fellow travelers in the Sierra Club, which was founded by John Muir. As a volunteer, David edited articles and wrote exuberantly about his mountain experiences for the *Sierra Club Bulletin.*

At that time, the Sierra Club sponsored summer "high country" trips. The tall, handsome, articulate Brower was a popular member of the mountain trips. The warm glow of his humor and his musical ability were natural ingredients of a happy campfire in the evenings. By bringing people to the mountains, the club was following Muir's expressed purposes to enjoy and appreciate the Sierras; preserving and protecting came later.

To earn a living Brower took a job with the University of California Press in Berkeley. A competent ski-mountaineer, he edited the *Manual of Ski-Mountaineering* for the university. It was during this job that he met his future wife, Anne Hus, who was also working as an editor in the same office. Their romance blossomed into marriage in May 1943.

These events were taking place as America was becoming involved in World War II. Brower served in the in the U.S. Army's 10th Mountain Division. He led several successful battles in Italy's high mountains.

After the war was over, he returned to his editorial job at the University of California Press. He enjoyed his work as a book editor, but it was as a Sierra Club volunteer that he had already started his life's work: saving the environment.

With the population booming, especially in California, the Sierra Club became concerned when the Bureau of Reclamation engineers proposed constructing ten hydroelectric dams on the Colorado River. The dams were supposed to appease the growing public demand for electric power. Sensing the coming battles, the seven-thousand-member Sierra Club hired Brower as its first executive director in 1952 to give full attention to these concerns.

The new executive director led the Sierra Club in opposing the dams on the Green River at Dinosaur National Monument. Brower developed a strategy that the club used again and again in later

David Brower believes that every person has a responsibility to protect the environment for future generations.

conservation battles. His plan included using full-page ads about Dinosaur in major newspapers such as the *Denver Post.* He also inspired people to lobby their lawmakers. He screened films of the Green River wilderness area (or any area under dispute), made speeches, sponsored boat trips down the river, and wrote magazine articles for national magazines such as *Life* and *National Geographic.*

Publishing powerful exhibit-format books came later. These large ten-inch by thirteen-inch books with stunning photos and eloquent text enabled many people to visualize what they could not actually see firsthand.

For the Dinosaur anti-dam fight, Brower directed the publication of the book *This is Dinosaur.* It contained beautiful photographs and articles written by several scientists describing the unique aspects of Dinosaur. Before the vote was taken to build the dams, Brower put this book into the hands of every member of Congress. He made several trips to Washington to testify before a congressional committee. By 1955, public pressure and an informed Congress helped to spare Dinosaur National Monument.

To environmentalists, the Dinosaur conflict demonstrated that environmental issues are political issues. To Brower, it confirmed that hard-nosed political clout and an informed public can take action and sway legislation.

Much to Brower's regret, in settling the

Dinosaur dispute a compromise was reached with the Sierra Club to build a dam downstream at Glen Canyon. That dam now backs up 186 miles of the Colorado River in southern Utah and northern Arizona. It covers two thousand miles of previously beautiful canyons, creating Lake Powell.

Brower repeated the full-page advertisement strategy to help rescue the ancient redwood forests in northern California. When the Sierra Club challenged plans for two dams for the Grand Canyon in Arizona, Brower again led an aggressive struggle to save it.[2] Flood the Grand Canyon? It reminded club members of the losses of the Hetch Hetchy Valley and Glen Canyon.

Brower produced another exhibit-format book, *Time and the River Flowing,* that showed magnificent photos of the Grand Canyon. When the government claimed that the lakes created by the dams would enable more people to see the canyon walls from boats, Brower's full-page advertisement in *The New York Times* asked, "SHOULD WE ALSO FLOOD THE SISTINE CHAPEL SO TOURISTS CAN GET NEARER THE CEILING?" Another headline warned readers, "Now Only You Can Save The Grand Canyon From Being Flooded . . . For Profit!"[3]

The ads and their warnings were timely and bold and they caused thousands of people to place pressure on Congress—again, the dams were not built. The Sierra Club lost its tax-exempt status because of its political actions, but its membership increased to seventy thousand. Brower and other members urged formation of the Sierra Club Foundation, which has tax-exempt status with the IRS.

After Congress passed Wilderness Act of 1964, Brower steered the Sierra Club toward using the courts to protect the environment. A historic court decision (regarding Storm King Mountain in New York) upheld the concept that parts of nature (canyons, rivers, lakes, mountains, old forests) could be represented and defended in courts.

After a conflict with the Sierra Club's board of directors, Brower resigned his position as executive director under pressure in May 1969. The club later awarded him the John Muir Award for outstanding service to the environment and made him an honorary vice-president.

In July 1969, Brower founded the League of Conservation Voters and Friends of the Earth (FOE). The goal of FOE was to inform, educate, and inspire people internationally to save the earth from all destructive practices, including the buildup of nuclear arms. Friends of the Earth has now expanded to fifty-one countries. Brower's insistence on book publishing as an educational force put him at odds with the FOE directors. He then resigned from the FOE Board.

When the use of nuclear technology became an ecological issue, Brower realized that environmental groups needed to encompass the entire planet. His answer was the founding of Earth Island Institute in 1982. He urged all organizations and individuals concerned about the ecological crisis to come together in the Fate and Hope of the Earth Conferences of 1982. A global focus on the environment—including human problems—was attempted when the United Nations sponsored the Earth Summit in Rio in 1992.

With Brower at the helm, Earth Island Institute now coordinates projects on six continents focused on cleaning up and restoring the planet. On his 80th birthday, David Brower declared, "I am dedicating the rest of my time to restoring what we've already spoiled. Now, it's healing time on Earth."[4]

Anne and David Brower have four grown children. When David speaks of his three grandchildren, he cites Thomas Jefferson's belief that one generation does not have the right to encroach upon another. He says, "They deserve a livable planet—once it is gone, it is gone forever."[5]

David Brower still has a remarkable ability to go beyond being a mere *observer* to being an *advocate*, and beyond that to being an *activist* for the environment. He often quotes a poster that hangs beside his desk showing a photograph of two mountain climbers on Mt. Everest. Under the picture it says, "Whatever you can do or dream you can, begin it. Boldness has genius, power and magic in it."[6]

Barry Commoner

Barry Commoner

"The Paul Revere of Ecology"

As Earth Day 1970 approached, *Time* magazine's front cover featured Dr. Barry Commoner. The article called him "The Paul Revere of Ecology,"[1] referring to Paul Revere's ride to alert the colonists about the approaching danger of British troops. For almost ten years, ecologist Commoner had issued warnings about environmental dangers such as radioactive fallout, the dangers of spraying DDT and other pesticides (expanding Rachel Carson's work), and the threat of polluted air and water.

In the late 1970s, an incident occurred that made people remember the title given to Commoner by *Time* magazine. During the Alaskan pipeline controversy, a nuclear scientist proposed using a nuclear bomb to blast a harbor in coastal Alaska. Commoner frantically warned government officials, the native Eskimos, and Laplanders of the dangers of the strontium 90 that would be released in such an explosion.

He pointed out that the fallout would float on air currents and land on the lichen that covered the area. Lichen grows not by roots and soil, but by absorbing dust from the air. When caribou ate the lichen, they would become contaminated. When native people ate the caribou meat, they would become ill and die.[2]

Because of Commoner's warning, the bomb was not used for this purpose. Like Paul Revere's alert, Commoner's warnings alerted the public and saved lives. The incident helped to highlight the use of science in adapting new technologies for public use.

Barry Commoner first knew that he wanted to be a scientist when his uncle gave him a microscope for his ninth birthday. The gift sparked his interest in the natural world, especially in plants. Barry, born in 1917 to Russian immigrant parents, lived on the outskirts of Brooklyn, New York. As a young boy, Barry soon found many specimens to examine under the lens.

His interest in science persisted through high school. He continued his education at Columbia University where he graduated with honors in zoology in 1937. Preparing for a career in science, he studied at Harvard University and four years later earned a doctorate in cellular physiology. He was in his mid-twenties when he took a teaching job at Queens College in New York, but his teaching career was cut short when he joined the U.S. Naval Reserve in 1942.

The Navy made use of Commoner's scientific background by assigning him to military research. His first assignment was to assist in the application of DDT, the new "miracle" chemical that had protected American troops from insect-borne diseases during the war. At that time, it was considered harmless to human beings.

Commoner discovered the side effects of the spray when a rocket station and surrounding water off the coast of New Jersey were sprayed with DDT to eliminate swarms of flies. Within hours the targeted flies were dead—and later, so were tons of fish![3] This demonstrated again that "pieces" of the biological world cannot be treated with a deadly poison, because the pieces are all connected through nature's cycles and food chains.

Commoner served as a naval liaison officer with the Senate Committee on Military Affairs, which was studying the role of science in legislating public policies. He realized that as a scientist he could provide relevant information to lawmakers when they were making decisions affecting human life and the environment. This became clearer to him as he investigated the fallout resulting from aboveground atomic testing.

The Atomic Energy Commission (AEC), formed

in 1946, was in charge of developing both military and peacetime uses for nuclear energy. Commoner was present when atomic scientists made their presentations on the possible uses of atomic power. He promoted civilian control—as opposed to military control—of the awesome power of the atom.

After the war ended, Commoner joined the faculty of Washington University in St. Louis in 1947. He did extensive cellular research and challenged the theory that DNA alone is wholly responsible for carrying all hereditary features. One of his major contributions was to develop new techniques for early detection of cancerous tissue. He was also responsible for milestone studies of the effects of radiation on human tissue.

By 1951 the United States had set off sixteen aboveground nuclear test explosions. The public was assured that the tests were harmless. In 1953, after a test in the Nevada desert, deadly iodine 131 and strontium 90 drifted into Utah grasslands. Cows ate the affected grass and produced milk that contained iodine 131, which became concentrated in the thyroid glands of the children who drank this milk. Strontium 90 also moved through the food chain and became concentrated in vegetables, in milk, and in people's bones. It usually caused leukemia.[4] After this discovery, Commoner wrote, "In such a closed, circular system, there is no such thing as 'waste'; everything that is produced . . . 'goes somewhere.'"[5]

After strenuous protests against nuclear testing,

Barry Commoner has spent much of his life educating people about the dangers of radioactive fallout, the spraying of pesticides, and air and water pollution. His warning about environmental dangers inspired a national magazine to call him "The Paul Revere of Ecology."

Commoner and like-minded scientists—plus an informed public—pressured Congress to pass the Nuclear Test Ban Treaty in 1963. The United States and the Soviet Union agreed to stop atmospheric nuclear testing. Thirty years would pass before the nations would be persuaded to stop underground testing as well. Commoner has noted that "humans pay a price for every intrusion into the natural environment."[6]

In January 1966, the Center for the Biology of Natural Systems was established at Washington University in St. Louis, Missouri. (It was moved to Queens College in Flushing, New York, in 1980.) The staff was drawn from many fields of study, such as biophysics, sanitary engineering, and economics.

Under Commoner's direction, the center became a major environmental research facility. The scientists generated solutions to problems dealing with the environment, energy, and natural resources. They later formed a Center for Environmental Information to keep both the scientific community and the public informed about environmental news.

Commoner's research on plants and natural cycles led him to caution the public that the present methods of sewage treatment were a violation of a fundamental principle of ecology. He warned that adding chemical compounds to sewage and putting it back into the soil and water upset the balance of nature.[7]

Because of Commoner's expertise as a scientist

and because of his personal pro-environmental philosophy, he played a key role in establishing Earth Day in 1970. New findings about pollution propelled the environmental movement to do work beyond the preservation of living rivers, wilderness areas, and old-growth forests. Environmentalists now added to the movement a vigorous campaign to stop pollution of the air and water by industry and agriculture. Like Ellen Richards a century earlier, they included the internal quality of homes and eco-friendly communities to their concerns. The polluted environment was being linked to cancer.[8] As in the 1960s there was a renewed interest in holistic medicine and healthy bodies, interests in line with the environmentalists' everything-is-connected outlook.

Meanwhile, scientists such as Commoner were drawing attention to the dying ecosystem of Lake Erie. It had become increasingly polluted and was almost lifeless from the dumping of industrial wastes. This tragedy served as an example of human failure to prevent environmental disaster. The lake is now slowly recovering because chlorine and other chemically-oriented wastes were banned by the National Environmental Policy Act of 1970. The stated purpose of the act was to prevent and eliminate damage to the environment and the biosphere. Using the Lake Erie example, Commoner cited the dangers of producing synthetic fibers, plastics, and chemicals. He stated, "Controls don't work. When a pollutant is produced, it's too late. . . . If you don't put something into the environment, it's not there!"[9]

Frustrated by the resistance he encountered while trying to get that message across, Commoner formed the Citizens party in 1980 and ran for president of the United States. He called for "environmental democracy," in which elected officials would make decisions benefiting both the environment and the common good. He received few votes during the election, but had the opportunity to raise fundamental questions about the environment.

In 1994 he summarized the indisputable lessons learned from past efforts to improve the environment:

- Efforts to recapture pollutants after they are produced have largely failed.

- To prevent pollution, stop it at its origin.

- A successful environmental program is an investment policy to transform industry, agriculture, transportation, and energy production along ecologically-sound lines.[10]

Today Commoner still lives in Brooklyn Heights with his wife, Lisa. They have two grown children and one granddaughter. He is a striking figure with his white, closely-cut hair, horn-rimmed glasses, and deep, husky voice. Now in his 70s, he still directs The Center for the Biology of Natural Systems, where the current focus is on waste disposal, that is, recycling versus incineration.

In his book, *Making Peace With the Planet,* Commoner documents how far short we have fallen of the eco-revolution challenges of the 1960s and 1970s. He feels that environmental pollution is an incurable disease unless we redesign our basic production technology in industry, agriculture, energy, and transportation. He calls for ecologically friendly technology. Commoner is called a socio-ecologist because of his outspoken views on social, economic, and political problems relating to the environment. He states, "To make peace with the planet, we must make peace among the peoples who live in it."[11]

Sylvia Earle

Sylvia Earle

"Her Royal Deepness"

Dr. Sylvia Earle, known by her colleagues as "Her Royal Deepness," was full of anticipation as she stepped into *Deep Rover,* the one-person deep ocean vehicle. She knew how the astronauts traveling to the moon must have felt. Sixty miles off the Pacific coast, she was going where no scientist, explorer, or solo diver had ever gone before—to the deep frontier.

As she closed the domelike top of the vehicle, she checked the control switches for *Rover's* mechanical arms. Earle then turned on the battery-powered thrusters as the research ship dropped her slowly into the frigid sea. It took an hour for her to reach the record-breaking, three-thousand-foot depth. On the way down, Earle spoke to the topside crew by radio, describing the sea life revealed by *Rover*'s lights. When she reached her destination in the deep wilderness, she turned off the lights and saw what she described as "deep-sea fireworks." The animals illuminated themselves as if on parade before her eyes. "I see a beautiful red octopus, a lantern fish, and a see-through octopus," she told the crew.[1]

She examined as many species as possible—some never before identified. Time seemed to evaporate. As she ascended, she wondered how many more species existed even deeper, in the deep gorges of the sea.

Sylvia had always had an unwavering curiosity about the ocean. It started early in her life during her family's two-week vacation each summer at the New Jersey seashore. The tidal-zone sea life was fascinating to her.

Born in 1935, she was thirteen when Lewis and Alice Earle moved from Camden, New Jersey, to Dunedin, Florida. The move allowed Sylvia to feed her curiosity as she used the nearby Gulf of Mexico as her own private laboratory.

She excelled in science and finished high school at age sixteen. At Florida State University, she continued her studies in marine biology, graduating in 1955. It was as an eighteen-year old biology student that Sylvia made her first scuba dive in the Gulf of Mexico. She immediately knew that she would spend her life working in the realm of the sea.

The next year, at Duke University, she specialized

in the study of marine plants. At age twenty, she received a master's degree. It was during this time that Earle began a distinguished ten-year study of algae's relationship to food chains. The research led to her doctorate from Duke University in 1966.

Earle learned that everything on earth, whether above or below the water, depends on plants. Life starts with the sun's energy, which is locked into plants through a process called photosynthesis. This was not a new idea, but she related it specifically to algae and analyzed the deterioration of plant life in Florida's Gulf waters, noting the damage inflicted by pollution.[2]

It is significant to note that one outcome of her studies was the idea for marine sanctuaries, which protect some of the ocean waters today. The U.S. Marine Protection, Research and Sanctuaries Act was passed in 1972.

As Earle studied the effects of pollution, she voiced her concerns about Florida's Fenhallow River being turned into a legal "open sewer." She was concerned about the Fenhallows's impact on river life and on the sea-grass meadows as it flowed into the Gulf. She saw creatures she had known as a child—sea horses, puffer fish, pink urchins, basket stars—diminish in numbers, and then disappear.

She also observed the damage to undersea systems caused by the dredging operations in Tampa Bay in the 1950s and 1960s. No one listened to her warnings about ocean damage.[3]

Earle realized that she would have to gain wider experience and become more knowledgeable in the field of marine science before anyone would hear her plea for the oceans. She knew that a major obstacle to ocean research, like space research, would be getting there—going deep enough to discover all the parts of the ocean ecosystem.

Earle joined a team of scientists in the Bahamas in 1968 where she experimented with a vehicle called *Deep Diver*. It was the first modern submersible (underwater vessel) with a lockout chamber permitting divers to leave and return to the vehicle while underwater. She was able to leave the vessel at various depths to study deepwater plants along a famous ocean cliff called Tongue of the Ocean. She was primarily interested in ocean ecology, that is, food chains or the balance between plants and animals.

Earle said, "How do we know what an unhealthy ecosystem looks like if we haven't seen a healthy ecosystem in that locale?"[4] For that reason, she either led or participated in numerous other research dives to study marine organisms and to do ecosystem analysis. Different localities included waters off the coasts of Panama, Chile, Ecuador, Peru, and Baja California; in the Indian Ocean; and in the Caribbean Sea.

In the 1970s, biosphere experiments were being conducted to find out how human beings would react to extended isolation in space and under the

As a respected marine biologist and author, Sylvia Earle educates the public about the need to protect the ocean ecology. One of her research projects led to the formation of marine sanctuaries, which currently protect some ocean waters.

sea. The United States government sponsored the Tektite I and II underwater research projects.

In the Tektite II project, Earle headed an all-female team of four other marine scientists living fifty feet underwater for two weeks near a coral reef in the Virgin Islands. The aquanauts lived in a four-room habitat composed of two towers. One tower contained a lockout hatch and support equipment. The other tower contained comfortable living quarters with warm showers and hot meals.

This type of "saturation diving" permitted unhurried observations. Earle classified and cataloged the plants in the area. Of the 153 species of plants that she observed, 26 had never before been seen in the coastal waters. She used her camera to document her discoveries. When the scientists emerged from their two weeks of isolation, they were hailed as heroes, given a ticker-tape parade in Chicago, and invited to the White House. The Tektite experiment had been a success both in terms of the scientists' proven ability to live underwater and in the data they gathered.

Tektite had provided Sylvia with a unique opportunity to introduce the public to the deep frontier because of her firsthand knowledge of ocean life. As Earle accepted invitations to speak of her discoveries, she used the opportunity to also deliver warnings about ocean pollution. In various articles and speeches she declared the responsibility all humanity shares to protect the ocean's incredible diversity of life. She said, "The ocean covers nearly three-quarters of our planet, and about ninety percent of all living things are found there."[5]

Since whales had always fascinated her, Earle was delighted to join other scientists in 1977 to study and observe different kinds of whales in their habitats. Photographer Al Giddings joined the team's voyage to the waters near Hawaii, New Zealand, Australia, South Africa, Bermuda, and Alaska. The whale project ended in 1980 with the making of a film, *Gentle Giants of the Pacific.* It contains scenes of Earle swimming with the humpback whales and commenting on their place in the ocean ecosystem.[6]

In 1983 Earle was invited to make the deepest solo dive ever made without a cable to the surface. She wore a redesigned "Jim suit," named after Jim Jarratt, the first person to wear a similar suit. It resembled a modern space suit.

For more than two hours, Earle walked on the sea floor and examined the sea life of the region. She was tethered to a submersible (named *Star II*)—but not to a surface ship. No one would have been able to rescue Earle if anything had happened to the tether line. The 1,250-foot dive broke all existing solo diving records. Her findings, along with Al Giddings' photos, were published in the 1980 National Geographic book, *Exploring the Deep Frontier.*

In 1990 she was appointed the first female chief scientist of the National Oceanic and Atmospheric

Administration. It is the government office that oversees the nation's waters, fisheries, and marine mammal program. In this capacity she was sent to investigate the Exxon Valdez oil spill in Prince William Sound, Alaska. The destruction of that ecosystem, from the whales and otters down the food chain to the diatoms and phytoplankton, was overwhelming. In addition, the lives of those who depended upon healthy sea life for their existence were changed drastically. She said, "How do you weigh the forever cost of this catastrophe? . . . in so many invisible ways the ecological balance in those waters has been changed forever."[7]

Earle was one of six international scientists chosen to study the massive oil damage in the Persian Gulf after the war in 1991. Where scientists measured as many as half a million organisms per square meter only a few years ago, now they found only half a dozen. Earle commented that "once something is gone from this planet, . . . we will never be able to bring it back."[8]

As a widely respected marine biologist and author, Earle has lectured in more than fifty countries. She has logged more than six thousand hours underwater, on more than fifty ocean research expeditions. Referring to her eloquent appeals for saving the ocean ecology, *The Radcliffe Quarterly* called her, "The Lorax Who Speaks for Fishes." (The Lorax was Dr. Seuss's character who defended the rights of trees that were being destroyed.)

Earle resigned from her government office in 1992 to help with the research for and testing of vehicles that would go even deeper into the ocean. She cofounded the Deep Ocean Engineering (DOE) company in San Leandro, California, in 1981 with Graham Hawkes, a marine engineer. Hawkes had redesigned the Jim suit, and created *Deep Rover* and a robot called *Phantom.* Earle dreams of exploring the depths in *Deep Flight* I and II, tetherless vehicles that will glide through the ocean at the four-thousand-foot depth. Unlike some environmentalists, she favors the use of technology as a positive means of "getting us there."[9]

Dr. Earle insists that we must use every means possible to clean up and restore health to the planet, especially the oceans. She says, "If we could get one thing right, it would be to understand our connection to all life."[10]

Frances Moore Lappé

Frances Moore Lappé

Linked American Diet With World Hunger

Frances Moore Lappé put a piece of East-West Lasagna on her son Anthony's plate and waited for his response to her newest recipe. Without hesitation, six-year-old Anthony picked up his fork and dug in. Frances breathed a sigh of relief. She knew Anthony would not hesitate to tell her if it did not meet his approval.

It was the early 1970s and she was the proud author of a small volume called *Diet for a Small Planet.* It sold over 3 million copies. The book resulted in a revolution in the way Americans thought about the links between their dietary habits, use of land, and world hunger. She wrote it because she was concerned when the experts said that we were coming to a time when earth could not support the number of people trying to live on it. There would be drastic food shortages.[1]

Lappé spent long hours searching for facts about global food supplies. She surprised herself with her findings about the relationship between eating meat and the use of land—the effects were felt on a worldwide scale. She discovered that "eating low on the food chain" (that is, eating grains, vegetables, and fruits) was a positive ecological decision with numerous health and environmental benefits. Lappé, like most people, had been taught in school to select foods from the four food groups for each meal. In challenging this concept, some thought that Lappé was challenging the American way of life![2]

The results of her research surprised Lappé. She had grown up in Texas where beef was a part of her family's routine diet. Although she was born in Pendleton, Oregon, her family moved to Ft. Worth, Texas, in 1945 when Frances was one year old. She was the only daughter of John and Ina Moore.

Her parents' volunteer efforts and participation in founding the First Unitarian Church in Ft. Worth greatly influenced Lappé. She still remembers her parents and their friends holding late-night discussions around the Moore kitchen table as they talked about local and world problems. She called it, "the hum from the kitchen accompanied by the familiar smell of coffee."[3]

She loved knowing that the grown-ups were

discussing big, important issues, even if they did not agree. She knew they were talking about things they deeply cared about, specifically how to improve the world. In the Moore household lively conversation was a way to test one's thinking. In later years, Lappé realized that what she had experienced was basic "citizen democracy."

After completing high school, she left home to attend Earlham College, a small Quaker college, in Richmond, Indiana. It was the early 1960s, and she was faced with making personal decisions about the United States' involvement in the Vietnam War. Also, at this time, the civil rights movement rose against racism and poverty. Race riots exploded in the streets of many cities. Searching for her place in the social milieu, she took a job in the Philadelphia ghetto. For the next two years she met poverty first-hand. Frustrated because she wasn't finding the "root causes" of scarcity, she decided to seek further training in the School of Social Work at the University of California, Berkeley, in 1968.[4]

Meanwhile, she had met and married Marc Lappé, who was working in the field of medical ethics. They made their home a few miles north of San Francisco in the town of Greenbrae.

While doing her research toward an advanced degree, Lappé became intrigued with the relationship between the American diet, land use, and hunger. She uncovered some startling facts about world hunger. While the world's experts talked only of scarcity, she had discovered the incredible waste built into the American meat-centered diet. She also found that eating meat to get the daily requirement of protein was nutritionally unnecessary. She stated, "My world view flipped upside down."[5]

Her research revealed that a vegetarian diet could replace protein usually obtained from meat with a combination of vegetables and grains. The findings led her to conclude that cattle are wasteful converters of grain to meat. She states, "I learned that for every seven pounds of grain and soybeans fed to livestock, we get about one pound back in meat on our plates."[6]

She started testing recipes combining vegetables and grains for protein (instead of meat), and put her own family on a vegetarian diet. Lappé found herself fighting what she termed the "Great American Steak Religion" when she tried to discuss her findings with others. Finally she decided to write up her discoveries in booklet form. Then, through a fortunate series of events, she met Betty Ballantine, the publisher of Ballantine Books in New York. Ms. Ballantine persuaded her to publish the booklet and it became *Diet for a Small Planet* (1971). It was revised in 1975 and rewritten in 1981. After the first edition of *Diet for a Small Planet* was published, the Lappé family moved to New York. Although Frances and Marc agreed on having a strong home base, they found themselves going in different directions. They divorced in 1977, then moved back to the San Francisco

Bay area and shared custody of their two children, Anthony and Anna.

Because of the success of *Diet for a Small Planet,* Lappé was invited to speak at various conferences, TV interviews, and talk shows. People seemed to think of her as "the Julia Child of the soybean circuit." At first glance her book appeared to be an alternative cookbook. She had to strive very hard to persuade the public to consider the more serious problems that her book addressed.

She continued her research, using U.S. Department of Agriculture figures. Lappé was one of the first to realize that cattle and livestock consume more than 70 percent of all the grain produced in the United States.[7] Moreover, she found that producing one pound of steak uses twenty-five hundred gallons of water—as much as one family uses in a month! Livestock production, including water for U.S. crops fed to livestock, accounts for about half of all water consumed in the United States.[8]

She discovered that corn and soybeans, the major animal feed crops, are linked to greater topsoil erosion than any other crop. Moreover, the soil washed from farmlands ends up in rivers, streams, and reservoirs, where sediments must be dredged at a tremendous cost to taxpayers.

Lappé persisted in her study of the economics and politics of environmental destruction caused by the U.S. diet. In 1977 she co-founded Food First (The Institute for Food and Development Policy)

Frances Moore Lappé and her husband, Paul DuBois, teach that the well-being and happiness of humans cannot occur without a healthy environment.

with Joseph Collins, a food policy analyst, in San Francisco. It was a research and educational program. From this platform, the institute launched studies that helped shift the debate about world hunger to a political and economic framework. Lappé and Collins studied the causes of hunger in countries where it existed on a large scale. They concluded, "Hunger, as well as environmental destruction, happens when access to land, credit and jobs is in the hands of a minority which is not accountable to the people."[9] They cited Brazil, in particular.

Lappé and Collins's book *World Hunger: Twelve Myths*, published in 1986, pointed out that hunger was a symptom of a much larger problem. It was not simply a problem of the land being unable to feed the growing population.

Environmentalists had first sounded the alarm about destruction of the environment by expanding populations following Paul Ehrlich's book *The Population Bomb* in 1968. Still searching for root causes, Lappé coauthored another Food First book, *Taking Population Seriously* (1988), with Rachel Schurman. Lappé and Schurman discovered that overpopulation, like poverty, results from a scarcity of democracy—particularly with regard to women being involved in decisions that affect their lives. They wrote, "We must learn to see ourselves as members of the interdependent biotic community."[10]

While working on the problem of how to empower people so that they become involved in the important decisions governing their lives, she met Paul DuBois. He is a prominent educator, social psychologist, and consultant to many service agencies, hospitals, and environmental organizations. Lappé and DuBois found that their ideas meshed and they established the Center for Living Democracy and moved from Greenbrae, California, to Brattleboro, Vermont. Their partnership culminated in marriage in 1991.

Lappé and DuBois are now consultants who teach people how to use the democratic process to solve local, regional, and national problems. They call it "doing democracy." In 1994 they published *The Quickening of America*. The book offers guidelines and training in citizen democracy as a pathway to change—whether the change is environmental, social, or economic.

They point out that when we begin to see the world through the lens of ecology, we begin to view ourselves in relationship to the whole web of life. We cannot seek our own happiness and safety apart from the well-being of the communities in which we live.[11] Ecological science is based on *relationships*. We understand this when we link acid rain to the health of forests—or link the destruction of rain forests to the thinning of bird populations in North America—or link pesticides on crops to the ill health of farmworkers and consumers. Lappé summarizes, "The environmental crisis teaches us what is true of all our social problems. The health of the whole is essential to the individual's well-being."[12]

Guide to National Parks

The philosophy imbued in the writings and actions of some of the environmentalists included in this book inspired the creation of America's unique 80-million-acre National Park System. The national parks are places of beauty for retreat and relaxation. The system, managed by the Department of the Interior since 1916, includes fifty-one national parks, in addition to national monuments, preserves, historic sites, and specifically designated areas, such as the White House.

The following list of national parks was compiled from online information provided by the National Park System. To learn more about the National Park System, visit its home page on the Internet.

ALASKA

Denali National Park and Preserve

P.O. Box 9
McKinley Park, AK 99755
907-683-2294
The park contains North America's highest mountain, 20,120-foot Mount McKinley. Large glaciers of the Alaska Range, caribou, moose, grizzly bears, and timber wolves are other highlights of this national park and preserve.

Gates of the Arctic National Park and Preserve

P.O. Box 74680
Fairbanks, Alaska 99707
907-456-0281
Often referred to as the greatest remaining wilderness in North America, this second largest unit of the National Park System is characterized by jagged peaks, gentle arctic valleys, wild rivers, and numerous lakes.

Katmai National Park and Preserve

P.O. Box 7
King Salmon, Alaska 99613
907-246-3305
Variety marks this vast land: lakes, forests, mountains, and marshlands all abound in wildlife. Here, in 1912, Novarupta Volcano erupted violently, forming the ash-filled "Valley of Ten Thousand Smokes."

Kenai Fjords National Park

P.O. Box 1727
Seward, AK 99064
907-224-3175
The park includes one of the four major ice caps in the United States, the 300-square-mile Harding Icefield and coastal fjords. Here a rich, varied rain forest is home to tens of thousands of breeding birds and adjoining marine waters support a multitude of sea lions, sea otters, and seals.

Kobuk Valley National Park

P.O. Box 1029
Kotzebue, Alaska 99752
907-442-3890
Here, in the northernmost extent of the boreal forest, a rich array of Arctic wildlife can be found, including caribou, grizzly and black bear, wolf, and fox. The 25-square-mile Great Kobuk Sand Dunes lie just south of the Kobuk River.

Lake Clark National Park and Preserve

4230 University Drive, Suite 311
Anchorage, AK 99508
907-271-3751
Covering four million acres, the spectacular scenery stretches from the

shores of Cook Inlet, across the Chigmit Mountains, to the tundra-covered hills of the western interior. The Chigmits, where the Alaska and Aleutian ranges meet, are an awesome, jagged array of mountains and glaciers which include two active volcanoes, Mt. Redoubt and Mt. Iliamna.

Wrangell-St. Elias National Park and Preserve

Mile 105.5 Old Richardson Hwy.
P.O. Box 439
Copper Center, AK 99573
907-822-5234

The Chugach, Wrangell, and St. Elias mountain ranges converge here in what is often referred to as the "mountain kingdom of North America." It is the largest unit of the National Park System and includes the continent's largest assemblage of glaciers and the greatest collection of peaks above sixteen thousand feet, including Mount St. Elias. At 18,008 feet it is the second highest peak in the U.S.

ARIZONA

Grand Canyon National Park

P.O. Box 129
Grand Canyon, AZ 86023
520-638-7888.

Located entirely in northern Arizona, the park encompasses 277 miles of the Colorado River and adjacent uplands. One of the most spectacular examples of erosion anywhere in the world, Grand Canyon is unmatched in the incomparable vistas it offers to visitors on the rim.

Petrified Forest National Park

PO. Box 2217
Petrified Forest NP, AZ 86028
602-524-6228

Trees that have petrified, or changed to multicolored stone, Indian ruins and petroglyphs, and portions of the colorful Painted Desert are features of the park.

ARKANSAS

Hot Springs National Park

P. O. Box 1860
Hot Springs, AR 71902-1860
501-624-3383, x640

Forty-seven hot springs flow from the southwestern slope of Hot Springs Mountain, at a temperature of 143°F. In the past the baths were taken as a therapeutic treatment for rheumatism and other ailments.

CALIFORNIA

Channel Islands National Park

1901 Spinnaker Drive
Ventura, CA 93001
805-658-5700

The park consists of five islands off southern California: Anacapa, San Miguel, Santa Barbara, Santa Cruz, and Santa Rosa. Nesting sea birds, sea lion rookeries, and unique plants inhabit the area.

Kings Canyon National Park

Three Rivers. CA 93271
209-565-3341

Two enormous canyons of the Kings River and the summit peaks of the High Sierra dominate this mountain wilderness.

Lassen Volcanic National Park

Mineral, CA 96063
916-595-4444

Lassen Peak erupted intermittently from 1914 to 1921. Active volcanism includes hot springs, steaming fumaroles, mudpots, and sulfurous vents.

Redwood National Park

1111 Second Street
Crescent City, CA 95531
707-464-6101

Coastal redwood forests with virgin groves of ancient trees, including the world's tallest, thrive in the foggy and temperate climate. The park includes forty miles of scenic Pacific coastline.

Sequoia National Park

Three Rivers. CA 93271
209-565-3341
Great groves of giant sequoias, the world's largest living things, Mineral King Valley, and Mount Whitney, the highest mountain in the U.S. outside of Alaska, are spectacular attractions here in the High Sierra.

Yosemite National Park

P.O. Box 577
Yosemite, CA 95389
209-372-0200
Embraces almost 1,200 square miles of scenic wild lands set aside in 1890 to preserve a portion of the central Sierra Nevada that stretches along California's eastern flank. The park has these major attractions: alpine wilderness, three groves of Giant Sequoias, and the glacially carved Yosemite Valley with impressive waterfalls, cliffs and unusual rock formations.

COLORADO

Mesa Verde National Park

Mesa Verde NP, CO 81321
303-529-4461
These pre-Columbian cliff dwellings and other works of early people are the most notable and best preserved in the United States.

Rocky Mountain National Park

Rocky Mountain National Park
Estes Park, CO 80517
907-586-1206
The park's rich scenery typifies the massive grandeur of the Rocky Mountains. Trail Ridge Road crosses the Continental Divide and looks out over peaks that tower more than fourteen thousand feet high.

FLORIDA

Biscayne National Park

P.O. Box 1369
Homestead, Fl 33090
305-247-7275
Subtropical islands form a north-south chain, with Biscayne Bay on the west and the Atlantic Ocean on the east. The park protects interrelated marine systems including mangrove shoreline, bay community, subtropical keys, and the northernmost coral reef in the United States.

Dry Tortugas National Park

c/o Everglades National Park
P.O.Box 279
Homestead. Fl 33030
305-242-7700
Fort Jefferson was built 1846-66 to help control the Florida Straits. It is the largest all-masonry fortification in the Western world. The bird refuge and marine life here are notable features.

Everglades National Park

4000l State Road 9336
Homestead, FL 33034-6733
305-242-7700
This largest remaining sub-tropical wilderness in the coterminous United States has extensive fresh and saltwater areas, open Everglades prairies, and mangrove forests. Everglades is the only area in the U.S. where alligators and crocodiles exist side by side.

HAWAII

Haleakala National Park

P.O. Box 369
Makawao. HI 96768
808-572-9306
The park preserves the outstanding features of Halcakala Crater on the island of Maui and protects the unique and fragile ecosystems of Kipahulu Valley, the scenic pools along 'Ohe'o Gulch, and many rare and endangered species.

Hawaii Volcanoes National Park

Hawaii National Park, HI 96718
808-967-7311
Active volcanism continues here, on the island of Hawaii, where at lower elevations luxuriant and often rare vegetation provides food and shelter for a variety of animals.

KENTUCKY

Mammoth Cave National Park

Mammoth Cave, KY 42259
502-758-2328

The park was established to preserve the cave system, including Mammoth Cave, the scenic river valleys of the Green and Nolin rivers, and a section of south central Kentucky. This is the longest recorded cave system in the world with more than 336 miles explored and mapped.

MAINE

Acadia National Park

P.O. Box 177
Bar Harbor, ME 04609
207-288-3338

The sea sets the mood here, uniting the rugged coastal area of Mount Desert Island, picturesque Schoodic Peninsula on the mainland, and the spectacular cliffs of Isle au Haut.

MICHIGAN

Isle Royale National Park

800 East Lakeshore Drive
Houghton, MI 49931
906-482-0984

This forested island, the largest in Lake Superior, is distinguished by its wilderness character, timber wolves, moose herds, and pre-Columbian copper mines.

MINNESOTA

Voyageurs National Park

3131 Highway 53
International Falls, MN 56649
218-283-821

Interconnected northern lakes, dotted with islands, once the route of the French-Canadian voyageurs, are surrounded by forest.

MONTANA

Glacier National Park

West Glacier, MT 59936
406-888-5441

With precipitous peaks ranging above ten thousand feet, this ruggedly beautiful land includes nearly fifty glaciers, numerous glacier-fed lakes and streams, a wide variety of wildflowers, and wildlife including grizzly bears and gray wolves.

NEVADA

Great Basin National Park

Baker, NV 89311-9702
702-234-7331

From the sagebrush at its alluvial base to the 13,063-foot summit of Wheeler Peak, the park includes streams, lakes, alpine plants, abundant wildlife, a variety of forest types including groves of ancient bristlecone pines, and numerous limestone caverns.

NEW MEXICO

Carlsbad Caverns National Park

3225 National Parks Highway
Carlsbad, NM 88220
505-785-2232

This series of connected caverns, with one of the world's largest underground chambers, has countless formations. The park contains eighty separate caves, including the Nation's deepest—1,593 feet—and fourth longest.

NORTH DAKOTA

Theodore Roosevelt National Park

P.O. Box 7
Medora, ND 58645
701-623-4466

The park includes scenic badlands along the Little Missouri River and part of Theodore Roosevelt's Elkhorn Ranch.

OREGON

Crater Lake National Park

P.O.Box 7
Crater Lake, OR 97604
503-594-2211

Crater Lake is world known for its deep blue color. It lies within the caldera of Mt. Mazama, a volcano of the Cascade Range that erupted about 7,700 years ago. Its greatest depth of 1,932 feet makes it the deepest lake in the United States.

SOUTH DAKOTA

Badlands National Park

P.O. Box 6
Interior, SD 57750
605-433-5361
Carved by erosion, this scenic landscape contains animal fossils from 26 to 37 million years ago. Prairie grasslands support bison, bighorn sheep, deer, pronghorn antelope, and swift fox.

Wind Cave National Park

R.R. 1, Box 190
Hot Springs. SD 57747
605-745-4600
This limestone cave in the scenic Black Hills is decorated by beautiful boxwork and calcite crystal formations.

TENNESSEE

Great Smoky Mountains NP

107 Park Headquarters Road
Gatlinburg, TN 37738
(Also in North Carolina)
615-436-1200
The national park, in the states of North Carolina and Tennessee, encompasses 800 square miles of which 95 percent is forested. World renowned for the diversity of its plant and animal resources, the beauty of its ancient mountains, the quality of its remnants of American pioneer culture, and the depth and integrity of the wilderness sanctuary within its boundaries.

TEXAS

Big Bend National Park

P.O. Box 129
Big Bend National Park, TX 79834
915-477-2251
Mountains contrast with desert within the great bend of the Rio Grande, whose grit-laden waters rasp through deep-cut canyon walls for 118 miles.

Guadalupe Mountains National Park

HC 60 Box 400
Salt Flat, Texas 79847
915-828-3251
Rising from the desert, this mountain mass contains portions of the world's most extensive and significant Permian limestone fossil reef. Also featured are a tremendous earth fault, lofty peaks, and unusual flora and fauna. Guadalupe Peak, highest point in Texas at 8,749 feet; El Capitan, a massive limestone formation; McKittrick Canyon, with its unique flora and fauna; and the "bowl," located in a high country conifer forest, are significant park features.

UTAH

Arches National Park

P.O. Box 907
Moab, UT 84532
801-259-8161
Extraordinary products of erosion in the form of giant arches, windows. pinnacles, and pedestals change color constantly as the sun moves overhead.

Bryce Canyon National Park

Bryce Canyon. UT 84717
801-834-5322
Innumerable highly colored and bizarre pinnacles, walls, and spires, perhaps the most colorful and unusual eroded forms in the world, stand in horseshoe-shaped amphitheaters along the edge of the Paunsaugunt Plateau in southern Utah.

Canyonlands National Park

2282 S. West Resource Blvd.
Moab, UT 84532-8000
801-259-7164
Water and gravity have been the prime architects of this land, cutting flat layers of sedimentary rock into hundreds of colorful canyons, mesas, buttes, fins, arches, and spires.

Capitol Reef National Park

HC 70, Box 15
Torrey, Utah 84775
801-425-3791
The "Waterpocket Fold," a 100-mile long wrinkle in the earth's crust, extends seventy miles from nearby Thousand

Lake Mountain to the Colorado River (now Lake Powell).

Zion National Park

Springdale, UT 84767-1099
801-772-3256
Colorful canyon and mesa scenery includes erosion and rock-fault patterns that create phenomenal shapes and landscapes. Evidence of former volcanic activity is here, too.

VIRGINIA

Shenandoah National Park

Route 4, Box 348
Luray, Virginia 22835-9051
540-999-3500
Shenandoah National Park lies astride a beautiful section of the Blue Ridge, which forms the eastern rampart of the Appalachian Mountains, between Pennsylvania and Georgia. In the valley to the west is the Shenandoah River, and between the north and south forks of the river is Massanutten, a forty-mile-long mountain. Providing vistas of the spectacular landscape is Skyline Drive, a winding road that runs along the crest of this portion of the Blue Ridge Mountains through the length of the Park.

WASHINGTON

Mount Rainier National Park

Tahoma Woods
Star Route Ashford, WA 98304
206-569-2211
This greatest single-peak glacial system in the United States radiates from the summit and slopes of an ancient volcano, with dense forests and subalpine flowered meadows below.

North Cascades National Park Service Complex

2105 State Route 20
Sedro Woolley, WA 98284
360-856-5700
North Cascades National Park contains some of America's most breathtakingly beautiful scenery—high jagged peaks, steep ridges, deep valleys, countless cascading waterfalls and about 318 glaciers.

Olympic National Park

600 East Park Avenue
Port Angeles, WA 98362
206-452-0330
This national park is a large wilderness area featuring rugged glacier-capped mountains, deep valleys, lush meadows, sparkling lakes, giant trees, fifty-seven miles of unspoiled beaches, teeming wildlife such as Roosevelt elk and Olympic marmot, and the most spectacular temperate rain forest in the world.

WYOMING

Grand Teton National Park

P.O. Drawer 170
Moose, WY 83012
307-739-3300
The most impressive part of the Teton Range, this series of blue-gray peaks rising more than a mile above the sagebrush flats was once a noted landmark for Indians and "mountain men." The park includes part of Jackson Hole, winter feeding ground of the largest American elk herd.

Yellowstone National Park

P.O. Box 168
Yellowstone NP, WY 82190
(Also in Montana and Idaho)
307-344-7381
Old Faithful and some ten thousand other geysers and hot springs make this the Earth's greatest geyser area. Here, too, are lakes, waterfalls, high mountain meadows, and the Grand Canyon of the Yellowstone—all set apart in 1872 as the world's first national park.

Chapter Notes

Chapter 1

1. Henry David Thoreau, "A Week on the Concord and Merrimack Rivers," *Walden, and Other Writings*, ed. Joseph Wood Krutch (New York: Bantam Books, 1962), p. 33.

2. Walter Harding, *The Days of Henry Thoreau, A Biography* (New York: Alfred A. Knopf, 1962), p. 181.

3. Thoreau, p. 345

4. Brooks Atkinson, ed., *The Writings of Ralph Waldo Emerson* (New York: Random House, 1950), p. 905.

5. Thoreau, p. 172

6. Ibid., p. 173

7. Douglas H. Strong, *Dreamers & Defenders: American Conservationists* (Lincoln, NE: University of Nebraska Press, 1971), p. 13.

8. Thoreau, p. 343

9. Ibid., p. 64

10. Roderick Nash, *Wilderness and the American Mind*, rev. ed. (New Haven, CT: Yale University Press, 1974), p. 93.

11. Henry David Thoreau, *Faith in a Seed: The Dispersion of Seeds* (Covelo, CA: Island Press, 1993), p. 4.

12. Torrey and Allen, *Journal of Henry David Thoreau*, 12:387, quoted in Douglas H. Strong, Dreamers & Defenders: American Conservationists (Lincoln, NE: University of Nebraska Press, 1971), p. 14.

Chapter 2

1. Edwin Teale, *Wilderness World of John Muir* (Boston: Houghton Mifflin Company, 1954), p. 311.

2. Douglas H. Strong, *Dreamers & Defenders: American Conservationists* (Lincoln, NE: University of Nebraska Press, 1971), p. 87.

3. Ibid., p. 67.

4. Ibid., p.75

5. John Muir, *The Mountains of California,* The John Muir Library (San Francisco: Sierra Club Books, 1989), p. 101.

6. John Muir, *Our National Parks,* The John Muir Library (San Francisco: Sierra Club Books, 1993), p. 272.

7. Tom Turner, *Sierra Club: One Hundred Years of Protecting Nature* (New York: Harry N. Abrams, Inc., 1991), pp. 44-45.

8. Ibid.

9. Muir, *Our National Parks,* p. 1

10. Turner, p. 48.

11. Stephen Fox, *The American Conservation Movement: John Muir & His Legacy* (Madison, WI: University of Wisconsin Press, 1986), p. 125.

12. Turner, pp. 66-67

13. Linnie M. Wolf, *Son of the Wilderness: The Life of John Muir* (Boston: Houghton Mifflin Company, 1945), p. 44.

Chapter 3

1. Robert Clarke, *Ellen Swallow: The Woman Who Founded Ecology* (Chicago: Follett Publishing Company, 1973), p. 116.

2. Caroline L. Hunt, *The Life of Ellen H. Richards* (Boston: Whitcomb and Barrows, 1912), pp. 7-8.

3. Hunt, p. 91.

4. Hazel Wolf, "The Founding Mothers of Environmentalism," *Earth Island Journal* (Winter 1993-94), p. 37.

Chapter 4

1. Teresa Rogers, *George Washington Carver: Nature's Trailblazer* (Frederick, MD: Twenty-First Century Books, 1992), p. 30.

2. Barbara Mitchell, *A Pocketful of Goobers: A Story about George Washington Carver* (Minneapolis, MN: Carolrhoda Books, Inc., 1986) p. 40ff.

3. U.S. Department of the Interior, National Park Service, Tuskegee Institute National Historic Site, 1994.

4. Rogers, p. 65.

Chapter 5

1. Aldo Leopold, *A Sand County Almanac: And Sketches Here & There* (New York: Oxford University Press, 1949, 1987), p. 129.

2. Ibid., pp. 129-130.

3. Ibid., p. 132.

4. Ibid., pp. 224-225

5. Ibid., p. 215

6. Susan L. Flader and J. Baird Callicott, *The River of the Mother of God and Other Essays by Aldo Leopold* (Madison, WI: The University of Wisconsin Press, 1991), p. 303.

7. John Muir, *My First Summer in the Sierra,* The John Muir Library (San Francisco: Sierra Club Books, 1990), p. 67.

Chapter 6

1. Rachel Carson, *Silent Spring,* 1987 ed. (New York: Houghton Mifflin Company, 1962), pp. 1-2.

2. Rachel Carson, "Letters from Rachel Carson: A Scientist Sets Her Course," (M.S. theme by Dorothy Thompson Seif) Rachel Carson Council, Chevy Chase, Maryland.

3. Rachel Carson, *Under the Sea-Wind* (New York: Simon & Schuster, 1941), p. xiii.

4. Rachel Carson, *The Sea Around Us,* 1989 rev. ed. (Oxford: Oxford University Press, 1961), p. xiii.

5. Rachel Carson, "Our Ever-Changing Shore," *Holiday Magazine,* vol. 24 (July 1958), p. 120.

6. Paul Brooks, *The House of Life: Rachel Carson at* Work (Boston: Houghton Mifflin Company, 1972), p. 233.

7. Carson, *Silent Spring,* pp.16-17.

8. Rachel Carson, "The Gentle Storm Center: Calm Appraisal of 'Silent Spring,' *Life,* vol. 53 (October 12, 1962), p. 105.

Chapter 7

1. David Brower, personal interview, December 12, 1992, at the Brower residence in Berkeley, California.

2. Ibid.

3. David Brower, *For Earth's Sake, The Life and Times of David Brower,* vol. I (Salt Lake City: Peregrine Smith Books, 1990), pp. 366–368.

4. David Brower, statement made at his 80th birthday celebration in San Francisco, June 29, 1992.

5. Brower, personal interview, December 12, 1992.

6. This poster was published by the Sierra Club in 1965. The quote is from the German philosopher Johann Wolfgang von Goethe.

Chapter 8

1. "The Paul Revere of Ecology," *Time* (February 2, 1970), p. 58.

2. Barry Commoner, *The Closing Circle: Nature, Man, and Technology* (New York: Alfred A. Knopf, 1971), p. 54.

3. Barry Commoner, *Science and Survival* (New York: Alfred A. Knopf, 1966), p. 23.

4. Commoner, *The Closing Circle*, p. 51.

5. Barry Commoner, *Making Peace with the Planet*, (New York: Pantheon Books, 1975), p. 10.

6. Douglas Strong, *Dreamers and Defenders, American Conservationists* (Lincoln, NE: University of Nebraska Press), p. 227.

7. Commoner, *The Closing Circle*, pp.181-182.

8. Commoner, *Making Peace with the Planet*, p. 30.

9. Pat Stone, "The Plowboy Interview," *Mother Earth News*, April 1990, p. 118.

10. Barry Commoner, "State of the Union 1994," article for the Institute of Policy Studies, 1994.

11. Commoner, *Making Peace with the Planet*, p. 243.

Chapter 9

1. Andrea Conley, *Window on the Deep* (New York: Franklin Watts, 1991), pp. 24-25.

2. Wallace White, "Her Deepness," *The New Yorker Magazine* (July 3, 1989), p. 50.

3. Sylvia Earle, "The Lorax Who Speaks for the Fishes," *The Radcliffe Quarterly*, September 1990, p. 3.

4. Sylvia Earle, personal interview, March 14, 1993.

5. White, p. 56.

6. Ibid., p. 58.

7. Ibid., p. 65.

8. Ibid.

9. Earle, personal interview, March 14, 1993.

10. Beth Baker, "Exploring the Heavens–Below, Sylvia Earle Championing Earth's Oceans," *AARP Bulletin* (February 1994), p. 20.

Chapter 10

1. Frances Moore Lappé, *Diet for a Small Planet*, 20th anniversary ed. (New York: Random House/Ballantine Books, 1992), p. 18.

2. Ibid., p. 14.

3. Frances Moore Lappé, *Rediscovering America's Values* (New York: Random House/Ballantine Books, 1989), p. xv.

4. Ibid., p. xvi.

5. Lappé, *Diet for a Small Planet*, p. 9.

6. Ibid.

7. Ibid., p. 89.

8. Ibid., p. 76.

9. Frances Moore Lappé and Joseph Collins, *World Hunger: Twelve Myths* (New York: Grove Press, 1986), p. 4.

10. Frances Moore Lappé and Rachel Schurman, *Taking Population Seriously* (Oakland, CA: The Institute for Food & Development Policy Food First Books), p. 14.

11. Lappé, *Diet for a Small Planet*, p. xxiv.

12. Ibid., p. xxvii.

Further Reading

Anker, Debby, and John deGraaf. *David Brower, Friend of the Earth.* New York: Twenty-First Century Books, 1993.

Brower, David, and Steve Chapple. *Let the Mountains Talk, Let the Rivers Run: Prescriptions for Our Planet.* San Francisco: HarperCollins West, 1995.

Douglas, William O. *Muir of the Mountains.* San Francisco: Sierra Club Books, 1994

Earle, Sylvia A. *Sea Change: A Message of the Oceans.* New York: The Putnam Publishing Group, 1995.

Faber, Doris, and Harold Faber. *Great Lives, Nature and the Environment.* New York: Charles Scribner's Sons, 1991.

Flader, Susan, and Charles Steinhacker. *The Sand Country of Aldo Leopold.* San Francisco: Sierra Club Books, 1973.

Henricksson, John. *Rachel Carson, The Environmental Movement.* Brookfield, CT: Millbrook Press, 1991.

McKissack, Patricia and Fredrick. *George Washington Carver, The Peanut Scientist.* Hillside, NJ: Enslow Publishers, 1991.

Reef, Catherine. *Henry David Thoreau, A Neighbor to Nature.* New York: Twenty-First Century Books, 1992.

Vare, Ethlie Ann. *Adventurous Spirit, A Story about Ellen Swallow Richards,* Minneapolis: Carolrhoda Books, Inc. 1992.

Wallace, Aubrey. *Eco-Heroes.* San Francisco: Mercury House, 1993.

Index